LIVING

THE LIFE NO ONE ELSE IS

EMBRACING THE SUNRISE:
A JOURNEY TO FREEDOM

NJERI MUCHUNU

WESTBOW
PRESS®
A DIVISION OF THOMAS NELSON
& ZONDERVAN

WestBow Press books may be ordered through booksellers or by contacting:

WestBow Press
A Division of Thomas Nelson & Zondervan
1663 Liberty Drive
Bloomington, IN 47403
www.westbowpress.com
844-714-3454

ISBN: 979-8-3850-2861-0 (sc)
ISBN: 979-8-3850-2862-7 (e)

Library of Congress Control Number: 2024913153

Print information available on the last page.

WestBow Press rev. date: 07/10/2024

CONTENTS

DEDICATION

This book is dedicated to the Father, the Son, and the Holy Spirit. Your love for me is the greatest gift I have ever received. I cherish You. You are my all in all. You have taught me how to experience perfect peace and perfect freedom in the embrace of Christ Jesus! Regardless of my past mistakes or shortcomings, You showed me that I am truly who You say I am: Your beloved! This realization has brought incredible healing to my life and helped me live a life of perfect liberty.

ACKNOWLEDGEMENT

To my dear husband Freddie, alongside our treasured children Ryan, Roni, and Roy, I extend my gratitude for your unwavering faith in me and your constant encouragement as I follow the divine path set for me. Your love, patience, and understanding have been invaluable in my pursuit of my divine path. I am blessed to have such a supportive family by my side. Thank you for being my source of strength and always believing in me. I couldn't have done it without you by my side.

To my esteemed spiritual father, Ibrahim Chingtok Ishaku, I wish to extend my deepest appreciation for the profound influence you have exerted over my spiritual development and everyday life. Your instructive lessons have illuminated my path and fostered growth in me that was previously unimaginable. Your unwavering dedication to illuminating God's word and demonstrating His teachings has ignited a similar passion within me. It's through your guidance that I've learned to confront life's trials with faith and reliance on God. The depth of my gratitude for your love and mentorship cannot be measured in words. Your influence has been a precious gift in my life that I will always value. The wisdom you've imparted, your uplifting words, and your guidance, have significantly shaped my spiritual and natural journey. I am blessed to count you as my guide and confidant. I will forever cherish your teachings in my heart, and strive to pass on the knowledge and wisdom you've shared. I pray that God's blessings continue to abound in your life.

My heartfelt thanks goes out to each individual who has offered me prayers, support, and motivation in various ways. Your encouragement has been a source of strength that has helped me overcome challenges and reach new heights. I treasure and appreciate you all.

May divine blessings be abundantly yours.

CHAPTER 1

THE JOURNEY BEGINS

Setting Forth on a Sacred Quest

Hello there!

I appreciate your decision to choose this book. It's not just a random selection but a clear reflection of your quest for a unique and fulfilling life—a choice that sincerely earns my admiration. I am humbled that you have chosen to join me on this journey. I hope that the content of this book will bring value and enrichment to your life.

Let me introduce myself as a first-time author. The divine intervention of the Holy Spirit urged me to write this book—an instruction eventually reiterated by many individuals, unaware of the divine communication I had received years before. I admit that my initial knowledge about authoring a book was minimal, yet the Holy Spirit provided ceaseless guidance during my journey. This book is not a reflection of me but rather a message from Him, aiming to liberate you from every shackle, enabling you to lead a life of complete fulfilment.

For years, I grappled with the elusive concept of liberty in Christ. It seemed to evade my grasp; it was a struggle I did not even recognize I was enduring. Life was unfolded in the shadows of others' expectations. I was perpetually chasing their approval, never deeming myself worthy of acclaim. This was no strange narrative; it was my reality, etched into my being since childhood. Affirmation was a rare commodity from my parents, a result of cultural norms rather than a lack of love.

Their encouragement and pride were rare, something I later realized was not because they lacked as parents. It reflected a pattern passed down through generations. They gave their best with what they had, following the example set by their own upbringing. It was not until I began my spiritual journey that I recognized a deep-seated desire for their approval and praise.

Far from holding any resentment, I truly admire and am grateful for the excellent upbringing my parents provided. They made sure we had everything necessary (basic needs, moral guidance, discipline, quality education) and they instilled in us the importance of hard work.

The message ingrained in us was clear and simple: study diligently, secure a prestigious job, and family life will consequently fall into place. My parents were diligent, ensuring we had access to a top-tier education and a foundation built on perseverance. However, life's tapestry is often woven with threads beyond such straightforward paths. Unseen, unloved, unappreciated—that's how I felt as their eyes seemed blind to my toils for acknowledgement. I strived tirelessly, yearning for a love that felt conditional on my achievements, which, in their eyes, never seemed quite enough.

The absence of celebration and recognition in my family spurred a void inside me that later manifested in toxic relationships, romantic and platonic alike, where I found myself used, time and again. It was the echo of my past. I was still chasing approval, still altering my values for the sake of acceptance.

My life was riddled with fear: fear of failure, fear of rejection, and fear of judgement. I lived in a constant state of anxiety, always seeking validation from others. My self-worth was tied to external factors, and my happiness depended on the approval of those around me. It was not until I hit rock bottom, surrounded by broken relationships and a deteriorating sense of self, that I realized the root of my struggles.

It was time to break free from the generational cycle and redefine success for myself. I embarked on a journey of self-discovery and healing, learning to love and accept myself for who I am, flaws and all. I let go of toxic relationships and surrounded myself with people who loved and supported me unconditionally—or so I thought. As I dug deeper, I discovered that I needed to love and validate myself first before seeking it from others.

This realization led me to reflect on how society's definition of success is often tied to external validation. We are constantly bombarded with messages telling us we need to look a certain way, have a specific job, or fit into a particular mould to be considered successful. The message was loud that, to be cool, you needed to drink large amounts of alcohol and go from club to club every single night. I had fallen into this trap, thinking that seeking external validation was the key to happiness and success. The only things I gained from this experience were drinking buddies and terrible hangovers.

I began to question why I was seeking validation from society. Was it because I genuinely wanted those things, or was it because I thought they would make me accepted and loved? The answer was the latter. Society's standards of success were not aligned with my values and beliefs, yet I still sought them out for the sake of acceptance.

As I continued on my journey of self-discovery, I started to redefine success for myself. I realized that true success is not measured by external factors but rather by my personal growth and happiness. This led me to enrol in different personal growth programs that were centred on Christ. All this time, I had accepted Christ as my personal Lord and Saviour, but nothing about my life reflected this choice. I would go for prayers on Friday night and then from there straight to the bar to enjoy the weekend with my friends.

Little did I know that this was part of the process. Christ knew me, and He needed to work on me just as I was. Honestly, I was hard of hearing, and I had to go through a lot of chastising from the Lord to finally get it. I had to be stripped of everything: my job, my friends, and even my relationship. It was a humbling experience, but it brought me to my knees and made me realize that I needed to fully surrender to Christ.

I started spending more time in prayer and reading the Bible. I also joined a small group of like-minded individuals who helped me grow spiritually. Through this journey, I learned that true success is not about material possessions or superficial achievements but rather about having a strong relationship with God and living according to His will.

As I continued on this path, I noticed positive changes in all aspects of my life—mental, emotional, and physical. The things that used to bring me temporary happiness no longer had any hold over me. Instead, I found true joy and peace in living a purposeful and meaningful life according to God's plan.

One of the most important things that I learned is the power of forgiveness. Through my relationship with Christ, I was able to forgive those who had hurt me and let go of grudges that were weighing me down. This not only brought freedom and peace to my heart, but it also allowed me to show love and compassion toward others.

When faced with challenges and struggles, I no longer feel alone or helpless because I know that God is always by my side. He has equipped me with strength, courage, and resilience to face any obstacle that comes my way. Even in moments of weakness, His grace and love never fail to lift me up.

My faith journey forced me to face my insecurities head-on. It was not easy, but it was necessary for me to realize that true success comes from Christ and is not defined by society's standards.

I have always been a hard worker and diligent in what I do, but I lacked direction and purpose. With Christ at the centre of my life, I started to see things in a different light. I began to understand that my talents and gifts were not for my own glory or success but rather to serve God's kingdom and bring positivity into the lives of others. This realization brought a sense of fulfilment and joy that was far greater than any material or external success could bring.

I started to dedicate my time and efforts toward serving others, whether through volunteering or using my skills to help those in need. This not only brought me closer to God but also helped me find a sense of purpose and fulfilment that I had been missing before.

What I will tell you honestly is this: it was a very painful process. It required me to let go of my pride, my desires, and my plans. I had to surrender the known for the unknown. No one understood me anymore, and ridicule beset me. Nevertheless, I held on tightly to God, knowing that He was the only one who truly understood me and had a plan for my life. Many laughed at me and mocked me because I was no longer chasing after the things that society deemed important. Little did they know, I was finally free from the constant pressure and expectations of the world.

I learned that true success is not measured by wealth, status, or fame but rather by our relationship with God and living according to His will. When we let go of our own desires and ambitions and instead focus on serving God and others, He blesses us in ways that exceed our wildest dreams. The best part is this type of success is not temporary or fleeting. It brings a deep sense of fulfilment and joy that cannot be taken away by external circumstances. It sustains us through difficult times and gives us hope for the future. Through this process, I grew stronger in my faith, learned to trust in God's timing and plans, and found true success and fulfilment in serving Him and living for Him alone.

My approval comes from Him. It may not have been the path I initially envisioned for myself, but I am grateful every day for the journey God has taken me on. I know that as long as I continue to put Him first in my life, He will lead me to an even more fulfilling and purposeful future. If you're feeling lost or unfulfilled, I encourage you to seek God and His plans for your life. Trust in Him and let go.

In the eyes of the world, I am not perfect, but in Christ, I am perfect. This realization has lifted the weight of perfectionism off my shoulders and allowed me to embrace who I am, flaws and all. It has also taught me to extend grace and forgiveness to others, understanding that we are all imperfect human beings in need of a loving Saviour.

Furthermore, knowing that God has a great plan for my life gives me comfort and peace in times of uncertainty or struggle. I no longer have to strive for success or validation from others because I know that my worth and purpose come from God alone. When I do experience success, it is not for my own glory but for the glory of God.

I encountered the transformative love of Christ. In Him, I stumbled upon true liberation—freedom untethered to the validation of others. His unconditional love filled the void left by years of seeking affirmation in the wrong places. In Christ, I was already approved, seen, and valued beyond measure.

This journey to liberty wasn't simple—it required me to confront the pains of my upbringing and the reality of my past relationships. Yet, in doing so, I found solace in Him who reassured me, 'You are enough'. Through Him, I learned that my worth wasn't predicated on achievements or the fulfilment of societal and familial roles but inherent in my identity as a child of God.

Now, I look back at the odyssey that led me here, grateful for every twist and turn. It is through my story's complexities that I discovered the profound truth of where true freedom lies—anchored in the love of Christ, beyond the fickle tides of human expectations and conditions.

I have come to understand that this journey toward true freedom is ongoing. It requires constant self-reflection and a willingness to let go of past hurts and harmful patterns. However, with Christ by my side, I am empowered to break free from the chains of seeking validation from others and instead embrace the unconditional love He has for me. In fact, this newfound sense of freedom has allowed me to live authentically, unapologetically embracing my unique identity and purpose. I no longer feel the need to conform or seek approval from others because I know that my worth is already established in Christ.

Beyond my personal journey, I have also learned that true freedom extends beyond just our own lives. As we embrace the love and acceptance that Christ offers, we are called to extend the same grace and compassion to others. This means breaking down societal barriers and loving our neighbours as ourselves, regardless of their backgrounds or beliefs.

In a world filled with pressure to conform and fit into narrow definitions of success and happiness, Christ offers us a way out—a way toward true freedom. As you embark on this journey, may you always remember that your worth and identity are not defined by others, but by the love and grace of our Saviour, Jesus Christ. I want you to boldly embrace who you were created to be. It is in Christ alone that you can truly find lasting freedom, unbreakable and unwavering no matter what challenges or obstacles may come your way. There is truly nothing more liberating than living a life fully surrendered to Him. I pray that you too will experience this beautiful journey toward true freedom. Keep pressing on, my friend.

The best is yet to come.

Many of you may be familiar with the biblical passage that declares where the Spirit of the Lord is, there is liberty. Regardless, this book presents this truth to you. This biblical wisdom grants you an undeniable entitlement to complete liberty. The concept of liberty refers to the freedom of living as God intended for you to live. It's about embracing a life that isn't dictated or limited by debts, obligations, or the need to justify your existence. It's about accepting yourself, just as you are because you are fully accepted by Christ. It means shedding the unnecessary pressure of bending to the will of others for their approval. What I am referring to is a life where external opinions have no influence or power over you or the course your life takes. The only judgement that matters is God's perception of you and your acceptance of who He says you are.

In this world, we are constantly bombarded with the idea that our worth is determined by external factors such as appearance, wealth, and achievements. The truth is that our worth comes from within, from knowing who we are in Christ and embracing our unique identities. This understanding liberates us from the pressures of comparison and competition with others.

Furthermore, true liberty also means freedom from fear and anxiety. In a world filled with uncertainty, it is easy to become consumed by worries about the future or past regrets. However, as followers of Christ, we are called to trust in His plans for our lives and find peace in His sovereignty. This does not mean that we will never face challenges or difficulties. Rather, we can have faith that God is in control and will work all things out for our good.

The world around us continually pressures us to adapt to certain ways of thinking and living, often in opposition to our core beliefs. When we refuse to conform, we often face isolation, sometimes even ridicule, particularly when it comes to expressing our faith and speaking openly about God's principles. More and more, it seems that confessing Christ as our Lord and Saviour is met with embarrassment and contempt, particularly in well-developed nations.

Increasingly, society and even some churches are pressuring us to accept the LGBTQI community as an integral part and condone their lifestyle, despite the conflict with many biblical principles. It's my conviction that the way to embrace this group is by introducing them to Christ, guiding them away from what I deem as detrimental influences, and delivering them from their demon oppression and bondage. Does love cover a multitude of sins? Yes, but it doesn't necessitate that we ignore what we consider to be sin. Just as we don't let murderers live in our homes, we should be consistent with dealing with sins of all sorts.

This book will challenge the system of manipulation that makes us feel fear and shame, and help us live lives of peace and freedom as we walk the path that God has set out for us. I will candidly discuss these issues because I live in the liberty that Christ provides.

To you, the reader, have you ever imagined a life where you can be who God intended you to be, free from the fear of societal judgment or the need to explain your life choices? I believe you purchased this book to lead such a life, free from the shame and stigma placed upon you by a society that condemns non-conformity. As a believer who has accepted Christ and is filled with the Holy Spirit, you are entitled to this freedom. However, if you are unaware of this God-given right and cannot resist the adversary, you may remain chained. The enemy is a thief who robs when no one is watching. Knowing that freedom has not always been my reality, it is my mission, having discovered the secret to absolute freedom in Christ, to share this powerful truth with you.

While you've read in the Bible and heard from many spiritual leaders, the concept of living a life of absolute freedom may seem like an unattainable goal. You may have even reached a point of disbelief, feeling as if your life is far from liberating. Your daily existence is filled with struggle and as one fight ends, another begins. You may question, "What kind of liberation is there for me?" or even dispute the reality of such a life. It's plausible that some written promises in the Bible are merely words to keep you from surrendering. Are those affirmations hollow or do they carry weight? You've seen men and women of God living lives of hardship, or you could be one of them. Your life is a never-ending war. Despite the constant struggle, you still urge your followers to trust in divine help, miraculous healing, and blessings even when they seem absent from your life. Living a life of complete liberty in Christ is a phrase that is certainly appealing, but does it hold any truth or is it just a comforting illusion?

I'm here to assert that the statement is entirely and unequivocally true!

Come, let us embark on this voyage together, guided by the Holy Spirit. On this voyage, I will reveal to you the secrets that have been concealed for so long. As a team, we will apprehend the thief robbing you of your joy and freedom and the Son of Man will set you free. Remember, he whom the Son of Man liberates is truly free. Revelations will be gifted to us, our vision will be cleared, marking the beginning of a fresh era.

Take note: the pages of this book are anointed and as you peruse through, involve your spirit and receive grace from the Holy Spirit needed to liberate you from shackles.

Savour the journey!
God bless you!
Njeri Muchunu

CHAPTER 2

UNSHACKLING THE SPIRIT

Understanding True Liberation

The concept of freedom in the Bible is profound and multi-faceted, touching on spiritual, emotional, and societal dimensions. The key to understanding biblical freedom is realizing that it isn't primarily about the absence of external limitations, but instead about being released from the internal chains of sin and death through Jesus Christ.

In the New Testament, Galatians 5:1 (NIVUK) states, 'It is for freedom that Christ has set us free. Stand firm, then, and do not let yourselves be burdened again by a yoke of slavery'. This verse encapsulates the idea that through Christ's sacrifice, believers are liberated from the law of sin and can now live in the freedom of God's grace. This freedom is not a license to live selfishly, but rather an invitation to walk in love and serve others.

Another aspect of biblical freedom is the concept of freedom from fear. In 2 Timothy 1:7 (KJV), it says, 'For God hath not given us a spirit of fear, but of power and of love and of a sound mind'. This verse reminds us that we are no longer bound by fear because we have been set free by Christ. We can trust in God's protection and provision, even when facing difficult circumstances. This kind of freedom allows us to live boldly and confidently in our faith.

But what about the freedom to make your own choices? As Christians, we are called to be obedient to God's will and follow His commandments. However, this does not mean that we lose our free will. On the contrary, through Christ's sacrifice, we are given the ability to choose righteousness over sin. We have been set free from the bondage of sin and can now make choices that align with God's desires for us. Galatians 5:13 (NET) reminds us, 'For you were called to freedom, brothers and sisters; only do not use your freedom as an opportunity to indulge yourself, but through love serve one another'. Our freedom in Christ allows us to choose love and service over selfishness and indulgence.

Moreover, the Bible also speaks about freedom from guilt and shame. In Romans 8:1–2 (NIV), it states, 'Therefore, there is now no condemnation for those who are in Christ Jesus, because through Christ Jesus the law of the Spirit who gives life has set you free from the law of sin and death'. As believers, we are no longer defined by our past mistakes or failures. We have been forgiven and made new in Christ. This freedom from guilt and shame allows us to fully embrace our identities as children of God without fear or shame. We can live in the freedom of knowing that we are loved and fully accepted as we are by our Heavenly Father.

This freedom also allows us to break away from societal pressures and expectations. In Romans 12:2 (NIV), it says, 'Do not conform to the pattern of this world, but be transformed by the renewing of your mind'. As believers in Christ, we are called to live differently than the world around us. We are not bound by societal standards or norms, but rather we are called to live according to God's will and purposes for our lives.

This freedom also extends to our daily choices and decisions. As followers of Christ, we have the Holy Spirit living within us who guides us and helps us make wise choices. Galatians 5:1 (NIVUK) says, 'It is for freedom that Christ has set us free. Stand firm, then, and do not let yourselves be burdened again by a yoke of slavery'. This means that we are no longer slaves to our sinful desires or harmful habits. We have been set free from these things through the power of Christ. We can live in freedom and make choices that align with God's will for our lives.

Living in freedom also means being open to growth and change. As we follow Christ, our minds and hearts are transformed by His love and truth. This transformation may require us to let go of certain habits or behaviours that were once a part of our lives. It may also challenge us to step out of our comfort zones and try new things. Nevertheless, through this process, we become more like Christ and experience true freedom in Him.

In addition to personal growth, living in freedom also allows us to have healthy relationships with others. When we are no longer bound by selfish desires or harmful patterns, we can love and serve others selflessly. When we are no longer in relationships because of what we can get out of them, then we are truly free. We are free from the need for validation or approval from others because our identities are found in Christ. This enables us to build genuine connections and community with those around us.

Biblical freedom includes the idea of being free from the opinions and expectations of others. Galatians 1:10 (NIV) says, 'Am I now trying to win the approval of human beings or of God? Or am I trying to please people? If I were still trying to please people, I would not be a servant of Christ'. When we are no longer concerned with seeking the approval of others, we can live in true freedom and purpose according to what God has called us to do.

This freedom also extends to our relationships. When we are secure in our identities in Christ, we can form genuine and healthy connections with others without being held back by fear or insecurities. Galatians 5:13 (NRSVCE) says, 'For you were called to be free, brothers and sisters; only do not use your freedom as an opportunity for self-indulgence, but through love become slaves to one another'. In other words, true freedom is not just about doing what we want, but using our freedom to serve and love others.

In today's society, there is often pressure to conform and fit into certain moulds or standards set by others. However, when we have a strong sense of identity in Christ, we no longer need to conform to the world's expectations. We are free to be who God created us to be and live out our purposes without fear or shame.

It is important to note that this freedom does not give us a license to do whatever we want, but rather it empowers us to make choices that align with God's will for our lives. When we understand and embrace our identities in Christ, we can confidently say no to things that may lead us away from Him and yes to opportunities that further His kingdom.

Biblical freedom also extends to our thoughts and emotions. We are reminded in Philippians 4:6–7 that we can bring all our worries, fears, and anxieties to God because He cares for us. This means that we don't have to be controlled by negative thoughts or overwhelming emotions. Instead, we can surrender them to God and experience His peace that surpasses all understanding. This freedom allows us to live in the present moment and not be burdened by the past or be anxious about the future.

Perhaps the most important aspect of biblical freedom is our relationship with God. Through Jesus Christ, we have been freed from the power of sin and death. We have been given access to God through prayer and can experience His love, grace, and forgiveness every day. This relationship with God is what gives us true freedom because it allows us to live in alignment with His will and purpose for our lives.

Ultimately, the message of biblical freedom is one of surrendering your life to God. It is about letting go of your own desires and plans, and trusting in God's perfect will for you. This can be a difficult concept to grasp, especially in a world that constantly promotes self-fulfilment and living for personal success. Don't be fooled though; true biblical freedom comes from living a life in total submission to God and finding your ultimate joy and fulfilment in Him.

In Galatians 5:16 (ESV), the Apostle Paul provides crucial insights into what Christian freedom entails: 'But I say, walk by the Spirit, and you will not gratify the desires of the flesh'. This succinct yet profound statement carries significant weight when deciphering the biblical notion of freedom. It suggests that genuine freedom is not found in indulging every want or craving, or accumulating material wealth, or attaining societal status. Instead, the freedom heralded in the Bible is emancipation from the dominance of these 'desires of the flesh'.

What exactly are the 'desires of the flesh'? How can we, as modern believers, walk by the Spirit and experience true freedom in our daily lives?

The desires of the flesh refer to your human inclinations toward selfishness, greed, and immoral behaviour. These are the impulses that lead you to seek immediate gratification, regardless of the consequences or harm it may cause you or others. They stem from your innate sinful nature, which is at odds with God's perfect and righteous will.

To walk by the Spirit means to live in accordance with the guidance and influence of the Holy Spirit. This requires a conscious effort to align your thoughts, actions, and attitudes with God's teachings and principles as revealed in His Word. It also involves surrendering your own desires and submitting to God's will for your life.

By walking by the Spirit, you are choosing to live a life of obedience rather than indulgence. You are choosing self-control over impulsiveness, love over selfishness, and righteousness over sin. This does not mean that you will never make mistakes or struggle with your fleshly desires. It does mean that when you stumble, you turn to God for forgiveness and strength to continue walking in the Spirit.

Walking in the Spirit also involves developing a relationship with God through prayer, worship, and studying His Word. As you spend time in His presence and seek His guidance, your heart becomes more attuned to His will, and your thoughts are transformed to align with His truth.

Biblical freedom also extends beyond the individual level. In John 8:36 (NIV), Jesus proclaims, "'So if the Son sets you free, you will be free indeed'". This statement highlights that true freedom can only come from a relationship with God through His Son, Jesus Christ. It is not a superficial concept that can be obtained through human efforts but an unmerited gift bestowed on those who believe.

This freedom in the Spirit also allows you to break free from the bondage of sin and the patterns of this world. Through your faith in Jesus, you are no longer slaves to sin but instead have the power to overcome it and live according to God's will. This means living with purpose and intentionality. It involves using your gifts and talents for God's glory and following His plan for your life. This may require sacrificing your own desires and selfish ambitions, but ultimately leads to true fulfilment and satisfaction.

My dear friend, at the core of biblical freedom is the liberation from the shackles of sin. The scripture elucidates that everyone is held captive by the propensity to sin, ensnaring us in a cycle of wrongdoing that segregates us from the true essence of life intended by our Creator. Jesus Christ, through His atoning sacrifice, has broken these chains, offering a path to redemption and the opportunity for a recreated relationship with God. This redemption is foundational, setting us free from past transgressions and empowering us to resist sin's allure.

The law, with its rigorous demands and unattainable standards, once highlighted the impossibility of achieving righteousness through human effort. In Christ, however, there is deliverance from the condemnation of the law. This is not to abolish the law but to fulfil it, to provide a freedom that respects and upholds God's standards out of love and gratitude, rather than obligation and fear. This freedom internalizes the spirit behind the commandments, allowing us to live by principles that reflect God's character.

Death looms as the ultimate consequence of sin, the final oppressor from which no person can self-deliver. Biblical freedom includes a remarkable promise: victory over death itself. Endowed with the assurance of eternal life, you, as a believer, can approach your earthly sojourn with boldness and purpose. The spectre of death no longer holds dominion; it has lost its sting, extending hope that permeates through the temporal boundaries of life.

Living in freedom according to biblical tenets does not mean a descent into moral relativism or antinomianism. Rather, it upholds a standard of holiness and righteousness that reflects one's allegiance to God. It is an ongoing process of sanctification, wherein the believer's life increasingly embodies the virtues and morals of the Kingdom of Heaven.

True freedom, then, is not just the absence of physical or societal constraints; it is a state of being that transcends beyond the material realm. It is a spiritual reality that enables you to live with purpose and fulfilment, empowered by God's grace and guided by His principles.

It may seem counterintuitive to some, but true freedom lies in submission. By submitting yourselves to God's will and following His commandments, you free yourselves from the destructive nature of sin and its consequences. This submission is not a form of oppression or limitation, but rather a pathway to true liberation. Society today has distorted and reduced freedom to indulgence and self-gratification. My friend, the pursuit of material possessions and personal desires often leads to emptiness and dissatisfaction. However, when we submit ourselves to God's will, our priorities shift from selfish desires to fulfilling His purpose for our lives.

Submission also allows you to break free from societal pressures and expectations. In a world that constantly bombards us with false ideals and worldly standards, being submitted to God means finding your identity in Him rather than conforming to societal norms. You no longer have to strive for perfection or validation from others, but rather find your worth and fulfilment in your relationship with God.

Finally, a life of biblical freedom cannot be passive or insular. It beckons you to be an ambassador of the same freedom that you have received, to stand against injustice, to advocate for the oppressed, and to contribute toward a society that mirrors the just nature of God. True biblical freedom, thus, has a communal aspect. We see it in actions that strive to liberate others physically, socially, and spiritually.

A life of perfect liberty is the ultimate expression of deliverance through the love and power of Jesus Christ. It is about breaking free from the most oppressive bonds that afflict humanity: sin, legalism, and death. It's an invitation to a life that honours God. This comprehensive liberty is an enduring promise of the gospel, offering a freedom that transforms you and the community, and ultimately, encapsulates the heart of the Kingdom of God.

CHAPTER 3

CHAINS UNSEEN

A Narrative of Spiritual Captivity

For God hath not given us a spirit of fear, but of
power and of love and of a sound mind.
—2 Timothy 1:7 (KJV)

You may find yourself yearning for the freedom that comes with walking in the path of Jesus—a freedom He assures His followers. Nevertheless, you might feel bound, unable to savour this freedom you so deeply yearn for.

Have you considered what might be preventing you from fully embracing the expansive freedom found in Christ?

The first step toward finding liberty in Christ is to accept Jesus Christ as your Lord and Saviour. You may be asking why it is important to accept Jesus Christ as your Lord and Saviour. Well, I believe that the most important reason is to rekindle your bond with God, which sin severed at the beginning of time. It is all about a relationship with God, who created you because He loves you. You are actually exactly like Him and He desires for you to come back to Him.

Many years ago, my initial attempt at salvation through prayer was misguided, aimed at erasing my past and convincing myself I could improve my life without divine assistance. This self-deception only led me back into a life marred by sin. Had I met my end during that period of transgression, would I have been welcomed into Heaven? That verdict rests solely with the Almighty, and yet, I harboured serious reservations about my fate.

Today, however, I know who I am and why I am here on earth. It was only when I fully surrendered and endeavoured to abandon my sinful ways that I experienced Christ's transformative power. A genuine yearning for the Holy Spirit emerged within me; I invited Jesus to dwell in my heart earnestly. This inner change did not go unnoticed—my family observed my transition from a person who was argumentative, brash, driven to achieve worldly success, and conceited, to someone infused with gentleness and empathy. Witnessing my metamorphosis, they too were drawn to seek God, with some finding salvation.

Embrace Jesus Christ as your Lord and Saviour and witness a life-changing transformation. My journey is proof of the miracles that can happen when you give your life to Him. Invite Christ in and not only will you receive the promise of eternity, but you'll be empowered to change, becoming stronger and reborn through His grace. Experience a purpose-driven life, one filled with His purpose, and find true freedom with Him.

Once ready, repeat this prayer after me.

Heavenly Father,

With a heart humbly surrendered, I come before You in prayer. I believe in the depths of my being that Jesus Christ is Your Son, sent to redeem us from sin and to bridge the gap between the divine and human. I trust in the truth of Romans 10:9–10 that 'if you declare with your mouth, "Jesus is Lord", and believe in your heart that God raised Him from the dead, you will be saved. It is with your heart that you believe and are justified, and it is with your mouth that you profess your faith and are saved'.

Today, I profess with my mouth and confirm in my heart that Jesus is Lord. I accept Him as my personal Saviour, inviting Him to occupy the throne of my life, guide my choices, and mould me in His image. Thank You, Jesus, for Your sacrifice upon the cross—the sheer manifestation of Your love for humankind. I am eternally grateful for Your grace that washes over my faults and failures.

May Your Spirit dwell within me, granting me the wisdom to understand Your teachings and the strength to live a life that is pleasing in Your sight. Help me to love as Jesus loved, serve as He served, and to foster a spirit of forgiveness and compassion in all aspects of my life.

I renounce the paths that stray from Your light and truth, and I commit to following the path of righteousness. I am reborn today in Your everlasting love—a child of God, an heir to Your kingdom, and a follower of Christ.

In joyful gratitude and with love that knows no end, I offer this prayer.

In Jesus's name, Amen

Even if you do not recite the aforementioned prayer and choose to continue engaging with this book, the Holy Spirit's presence woven within its passages may still touch your spirit. However, be forewarned: choosing to experience this freedom without Christ is perilous. Forgoing His shield invites Satan to exploit your vulnerabilities. It is crucial to recall that true, perfect liberty is found only in communion with Christ.

Now, let us continue from where we left off.

The journey toward spiritual growth can be tough, marked by the challenges of self-doubt and external distractions. This chapter delves into the ironic struggle believers face between experiencing freedom as promised in Christ and feeling bound by negative emotions. We will take a detailed look at how fear and shame can hinder our progress and sense of freedom as we strive to walk in harmony with Christ's teachings.

A SHADOW OF FEAR

Throughout history, fear has often overshadowed freedom's bright potential. It wraps itself tightly around our hearts, filling us with worries and doubts. Fear presents the threat of loss, negative judgment, and feelings of inadequacy, causing even the most devout Christian to pause, weighed down by the heavy 'what-ifs' and potential outcomes.

Yet, Paul's message to Timothy stands as a timeless reminder that fear is an intruder. It's something we were never meant to carry. Rather, we are meant to embody the power, love, and self-control that Jesus grants to His followers. Fear is not from God; it comes from Satan, the father of lies.

THE STAIN OF SHAME

Shame and fear often weave together, creating a painful feeling that makes us hyper-aware of our past mistakes and current flaws. This feeling constantly tells us we're beyond forgiveness, convincing us our missteps are too great to be forgiven. Yet, this is how shame tricks us: by making us see ourselves as irredeemably flawed, ignoring the way God views us. It overlooks the truth that we've been forgiven and made clean, preferring to believe we're permanently marked by our errors.

GENESIS OF THE GOLIATHS

Fear and shame first emerged in the story of Adam and Eve in Eden. These feelings were unknown to them until they disobeyed, which revealed their mistakes and brought fear and shame into the world. These emotions, originating from that first act of disobedience, remind us of a paradise lost and continue to affect us today. They continue to challenge us, as they have since the beginning of human history.

UNSHACKLING THE CHAINS

However, all is not lost. For those weighed by their invisible chains, the key to the padlock lies in Christ and His Word, where instruction and assurance fan the flames of hope. With dedication and introspection, we will uncover and challenge the hidden truths behind their spiritual immurement.

The next chapter will serve as a foundation as we walk together to disarm the debilitating power of fear and silence the accusing voice of shame instigated by Satan. Through scriptural wisdom and practical advice, I aim to lay the foundations for the sturdy reconstruction of your personal Jericho walls, without the looming threat of their tumbling down once more. We will venture back to the roots in Genesis to understand the origin of our chained condition. Just as important, we will chart a way forward, developing a battle plan against the ancient adversary.

THE PROMISE FULFILLED

Our ultimate goal is no meagre feat. Each word you peruse, each concept you entertain is another steady chisel chipping away at the edifice of oppression. Gradually, the weight lifts, and light pierces through the once impermeable darkness of bondage.

My friend, take heart and courage from this next chapter, for it is both your map and your compass in navigating the odyssey toward the fullness of freedom in Christ. Truth is a mighty liberator, and knowledge its resounding sword. Join me in piercing the veil, and step forward, and upward, into the uninhibited glory of a life truly set free.

CHAPTER 4

GENESIS OF FEARS

How Terror Finds Its Roots

The foundational stories of Genesis have long served as a reference point for understanding human nature and the complexities of human emotions. The Bible tells us that we should follow the ancient paths of our ancestors, to find wisdom and insight into our own lives.

Let us explore the birth of two powerful emotions (fear and shame) as described in the book of Genesis.

The story of Adam and Eve is perhaps one of the most well-known stories from the Bible. It tells us how God created the first man and woman, placing them in a beautiful garden with everything they could ever need or want. Yet, despite having it all, they still succumbed to temptation and ate from the forbidden tree of knowledge of good and evil. This act led to their expulsion from paradise and marked the beginning of human suffering.

Before they were banished from Eden, something else happened that would have lasting effects on humanity: the birth of fear and shame.

Before the fall, Adam and Eve lived without fear or shame until the moment they ate from the Tree of Knowledge of Good and Evil, in direct disobedience to God's instructions.

UNDERSTANDING FEAR

I once lived a life of lying to myself, saying I wasn't afraid. Why fear when I had faith in the Lord? Yet, behind my confident words, fear was my constant companion, unknown even to me.

I thought I could predict every twist of fate, guarding against unexpected challenges. Fear secretly guided my actions, pretending to protect me. In reality, it built walls that only isolated me.

My every move was planned, and spontaneity became a ghost I avoided. Fear's grasp reached deep, turning my prayers from trust to doubt in the things unseen.

I held on to control like a shield, trying to stop the swift charge of uncertainty. In my own story, I was both the protector and the enemy, lost in the shadows of my making. My prayers echoed around me, filled with the sounds of a soul caught in worry's snare.

The illusion of control was a lovely yet confining shackle. I carefully made plans, teetering between thoughtful strategy and a paralyzing need for clear direction. I wanted to be in charge because if I was, then the outcome was predictable: it would be an overwhelming success. Why lie? Living life like this was always extremely exhausting, being the solution to many people's problems, not empowered by Christ, but driven by fear. I knew that if I had the answer, I would have power over them.

Eventually, reality shattered my makeshift security. My attempts to direct destiny plunged me further into confusion. The defences I had built were suffocating my soul.

At my breakpoint, clarity broke through—a resounding realization that no one can control life's unpredictable course. True faith was walking into the unknown, trusting that God knows all and that He loves me. What may be unknown to me is known to Him. I need not fear. Jesus did not leave me comfortless. All I need to do is totally surrender to His leading.

My prayers changed, from bargaining to peaceful surrender, submission, and acceptance. I realized my fears were transient travellers in life's journey. Each morning marked my step into true belief, not in my plans but in God's hand leading me through life's uncertainties.

Fear was meant to hold me captive with a distorted view of life's vastness. On the other hand, complete submission and faith in God guided me into embracing the adventure into the unknown, unafraid of storms and free from the facade of power.

In the flickering shadows of a world marred by doubt and insecurity, fear has become a common inhabitant in the inner chambers of human hearts. Many, even those who have professed their faith in Christ, find themselves ensnared by invisible yet profoundly constricting chains. Yet, they have no clue that they are bound by them. Many would even go as far as stating with conviction, 'I am not afraid'.

The roots of fear are ancient, twisted deep into the earliest chapters of human history. In the lushness of Eden, where humanity first walked in harmony with their Creator, fear was an alien concept. Only when humans trespassed against God's instructions did fear, like a parasitic vine, find its way into the human soul. The serene garden's atmosphere turned foreign as Adam and Eve felt an emotion unknown to them before (fear), that led them to hide from the One who had made them. This nascent fear compelled concealment, deception, and ultimately, a chasm between God and humans. Adam and Eve became aware of their vulnerability and nakedness, which led to feelings of shame and fear. This marked the beginning of the human struggle with fear.

The tremors of that fateful choice have echoed through the ages, shaping lives and destinies across time.

Even within those who follow Christ, a discipleship marked by the presence of fear is akin to a bird that, though free from the cage, remains perched within, too terrified to venture out. Fear does not discriminate between the faithful and the sceptic; it perpetually seeks to oppress, dominate, and control.

Real-life examples abound, such as the talented musician whose fear of failure prevents him or her from stepping onto the stage, silencing the songs meant to be shared with the world. Consider the gifted writer, plagued by the dread of rejection, whose stories gather dust, untold and unread. What commonality binds these examples? It is a bondage of potential, shackled by the cold iron of fear.

You may be saying to yourself, *I do not have fear. This is not me she is talking about.* How can you discern the presence of fear in your life? It is by recognizing its symptoms: hesitation in making decisions, constant expectation of catastrophe, or avoidance of relationships for fear of pain.

Consider this scenario: your adult children, over eighteen, request a night out with friends. You decline, not because of the destination's safety but out of a deep-seated fear for their well-being beyond your safeguard. This reflects a belief that only you can shield them and that they lack the judgement to differentiate right from wrong.

Let me share the subtle and not-so-subtle signs that someone is living out a story constrained by fear. Recognizing these signs is the first step in breaking free from fear by the grace of God and stepping out in courage and freedom.

I will share scenarios under each sign that will help uncover fear. Once the thief is caught, he can no longer steal from you.

1. HESITATION TO PURSUE NEW OPPORTUNITIES

Alex has been nurturing a side hustle (developing a mobile app) while working a full-time corporate job. His app has started gaining traction, and there's a real opportunity to pursue it full-time and seek investors. Despite the potential, Alex hesitates to leave his stable job and benefits, fearing the instability of entrepreneurship.

Worries about financial security and potential business failure hold Alex back from taking a chance on his innovation. The spirit of fear is evident as Alex struggles to step out of his comfort zone and chase an opportunity that could bring unforeseen success.

2. AVOIDANCE OF SOCIAL SITUATIONS

Linda hears about the high school reunion and the buzz it's creating among her old classmates. Yet, instead of feeling nostalgic, she feels paralyzed by the idea of being assessed or having to measure up to her peers' accomplishments.

Linda decides to stay away, missing the chance to reconnect and share in the collective memories.

3. PROCRASTINATION AND PERFECTIONISM

Taylor, a university student, is tasked with a report that accounts for 40 percent of the term's grade. Taylor strives for a flawless report to maintain a high GPA but is haunted by the fear of making mistakes. Taylor procrastinates on starting the report, waiting for the perfect moment when she feels knowledgeable and confident enough to write flawlessly.

However, the fear of falling short of perfection leads to a continuous cycle of procrastination. It's the night before submission, and Taylor is forced to write the report in a state of panic. While Taylor manages to submit the report on time, the quality suffers due to the last-minute rush.

4. Obsessive Worrying and Negative Predictions

Ever since becoming a parent, Emily can't stop worrying about her child's safety. She pictures all the potential accidents that could occur at school or on the playground.

She finds herself making negative predictions about her child's future based on normal, everyday risks, and it begins to interfere with her ability to enjoy her time as a parent.

5. Difficulty Expressing True Feelings

Rachel suffers from anxiety and depression but feels encapsulated by the stigma surrounding mental health. Wanting to reach out for support, she is petrified that her struggles will be dismissed or, worse, that she'll be viewed as weak.

Confiding in a friend could be a lifeline, but as they chat casually, the spirit of fear suffocates her pleas for help. Rachel's smile masks a silent battle, and her cry for help fades before it can reach the surface.

6. Reluctance to Leave the Comfort Zones

We all have a tendency to stay within our comfort zones, much like the Israelites who yearned for Egypt when faced with the uncertainties of their journey toward the Promised Land. It can be scary and uncomfortable to venture into the unknown, but it is through these experiences that we can truly grow and fulfill our purposes in Christ. Just like Abraham, who had to leave his familiar surroundings and journey toward the land of Canaan, we too must be willing to let go of our fears and step out in faith.

Stepping out of our comfort zones can also allow us to see God's hand at work in our lives. When we limit ourselves to what is comfortable and familiar, we may miss the amazing plans and blessings that God has in store for us. By stepping into the unknown, we open ourselves up to new opportunities and experiences that can help us reach our full potential.

PHYSICAL SYMPTOMS OF FEAR

Fear is a common part of human existence; it's an emotion that can both protect and limit us. Like a storm, it can sometimes feel overwhelming, manifesting not just mentally but physically. Recognizing this is a crucial step in navigating through difficulties and finding your path to perfect peace.

Let's be clear: there is absolutely no shame in admitting that you struggle with fear.

This section aims to provide you with valuable information to help you identify physical manifestations of fear in your own life. More importantly, it will guide you in seeking help on your path to deliverance through Christ.

Fear is a snare, as the Bible mentions in Proverbs 29:25. It confines many areas of life and those ensnared by it grapple with the following.

- **Decisions**: Fear magnifies the consequences of making the wrong choice, leading to indecision and stalemate resembling the wavering man in James 1:6–8.
- **Relationships**: Trust issues and fear of abandonment can derail relationships, much like the divisions caused by a lack of love as in 1 John 4:18.
- **Admission that you need help**: Admitting that you need help requires confessing vulnerability, which fear resists. This is in contrast to the biblical invitation to seek help in Hebrews 4:16, which says that we should draw near to Christ and find grace in our time of need.
- **Chronic Stress and Anxiety**: Fear unceasingly causes stress and anxiety, poisoning one's well-being and health. Matthew 6:34 warns against this.
- **Self-expression and Creativity**: Fear suppresses creativity and self-expression, restraining you in the same way the truth was suppressed in Romans 1:18.

- **Personal and Professional Goals**: Fear can block one's aspirations in the same way the Israelites were initially fearful of entering the Promised Land in Numbers 13.

Recognizing your entrapment by fear is a pivotal revelation in your life's narrative. However, God's Word encourages us that He has not given us spirits of fear, but of power, love, and sound mind (2 Timothy 1:7 KJV). By confronting and conquering your fears by the power of the Holy Spirit, you fling open the door to new chapters brimming with growth, interactions, and limitless potential.

Remember, every Bible story involves overcoming trials, and your life's story is no different. Don't permit fear to write your pages. Ask for grace to help you take control of your narrative, and choose to live fearlessly. Whether in the biblical narratives or in life, the most inspiring stories are those of victory over fear.

Always remember this: fear is more than an emotion; it is a spirit. When fear takes root, it cracks open the soul's defenses, allowing darkness to seep in. Each unchecked fear is an invitation, an entry point for sin and oppression by the enemy. It cripples faith, corrodes hope, and poisons love. However, fear's power is not ultimate. Therein lies the beautiful paradox— fear is rendered powerless when faced head-on with the unshakeable truth of the Gospel. When you abide in Christ, you are no longer a slave to fear, but a child of God who has been given a spirit of power, love, and sound mind (2 Timothy 1:7 KJV).

BREAKING FREE FROM FEAR'S GRIP

The struggle is real, and the process is often painstakingly slow, but the weapons are clear and victory is assured for those who wield them. Scripture immerses us in the powerful love of God—a love that 'drives out fear' according to 1 John 4:18. We learn to replace lies with truth, despair with hope, and paralysis with action grounded in faith. *To defeat the devil, you must defy the devil.* Counter his every attack with the opposite response. If he tells you to go left, turn right. If he whispers to you that you are not loved, remind him that the Lord Jesus loved you to the extent that He gave up His life for you even when you were yet a sinner.

Here are some practical steps.

- See fear as an opportunity for faith, each moment of anxiety transformed into prayer and calling on the Holy Spirit, your ever-present help in time of need.
- Cultivate a spirit of power—not your power but the power of the Holy Spirit, and recognize your identity as a child of God, equipped with divine strength.
- Nurture love for others, knowing that perfect love is the antidote to fear.
- Exercise self-control, for fear thrives in the vacuum of indiscipline.

This chapter has laid bare the roots and realities of fear. It has examined how easily the faithful can be caught in the snare of fear, despite divine reassurance. We cannot ignore this struggle, for it is the battleground upon which many spiritual wars are waged. Take courage, for every chain has a key. For the one that fear has forged, that key is faith, wielded with unwavering certainty in the One who has called us to be more than conquerors.

We will talk about fear once we tie everything together toward the end of this book. For now, may you step forward with a heart armoured by faith, eyes fixed on God, and a spirit liberated from the deceptive whispers of fear. With each act of trust, each prayer of defiance against the lies of fear, may you echo the triumph that echoes throughout the scriptures and reverberates in the testimony of saints across centuries: fear has lost its grip, and freedom has won.

CHAPTER 5

THE GENESIS OF DISGRACE

Unveiling the Origins of Shame

It was a sweltering Florida day in 2014 when the unforgiving sun poured its heat on the bustling pathways of Disney World. Families, children, and friends gathered, laughing and forming an endless sea of excitement. That mixture of thrill and anticipation saturated the air as I stood in line for one of the famed roller coasters, my heartbeat keeping time with the tick of the passing minutes.

My son was my world, and since bringing him into mine, I hadn't had much time to reflect on the shifts in my body. Adjusting to motherhood came with its battles, and my own self-image had admittedly retreated to the backlines.

The line shuffled forward, and I advanced with it, each step a march closer to the zenith of fun this ride promised. At last, I reached the gleaming metal beast, and its seats awaited their riders—containers of joy yet to unfold. It was my turn. I approached the seat as those before me had done. With a smile from the attendant, I attempted to settle in.

However, fate dealt a hand of cruel misfortune. The seat, a fierce jury, would not yield to accommodate me. A flush of red rose to my cheeks as the attendant tried to assist me, but the safety restraints were unyielding. Murmurs brushed my ears, and eyes glinted with curiosity and pity. The verdict was in; flanked by the silent gavel of the coaster seat, I faced the unthinkable.

'I'm so sorry', the attendant whispered, with a look that conveyed empathy yet scorched like acid.

I was asked to vacate the seat as a growing audience of strangers watched the unravelling of my private struggle in this most public of theatres. Every ounce of my being quivered with the weight of shame far heavier than any physical burden. Tears welled up, blurring the vibrancy of the park into an impressionist's nightmare.

The walk of shame away from the coaster's clutches was a lonesome march amidst a carnival. I hated myself then, despised the figure reflected in each glossy surface and every curious eye. In my head echoed a cacophony of unworthiness for the space I occupied, for the weight I carried post-pregnancy—a weight far more complex than mere physicality.

Humiliated, angry sobs clawed out as I sought refuge from a thousand prying gazes. I wished to vanish into thin air, to be nothing more than a whisper on the wind that might be easily forgotten.

That day, the clash of happiness and heartbreak crowned me in a twisted coronation. Nevertheless, within the tale is woven a tender thread of resolve—a silent promise to rise from the ashes of a momentary defeat. It's a story worn like a scar, a harsh lesson in self-forgiveness, a wound that compelled healing.

It was not only the seat at Disney World that I couldn't fit into. It was my own skin, a life reshaped by maternity. Yet, as the sun set over the magical kingdom, I grasped at the promise of dusk; the shadows cast were not just of the present, but of a past and eventually, they would yield to a new day, filled with the light of understanding and acceptance.

The emotion of shame is deep-seated and universal, touching the lives of every human being at some point. For you who seek to grow in your faith in Christ and experience perfect liberty, understanding the roots of shame, particularly its origin as described in the Book of Genesis, is a profound step in the healing process.

The Book of Genesis, the first book of the Bible, chronicles the creation of the world and the dawn of humanity. Within its pages, we encounter the inception of shame, tightly woven into the narrative of Adam and Eve. In the Garden of Eden, God gave Adam and Eve everything they needed to live in perfect harmony with Him and each other. In Genesis 2, Adam and Eve lived in the Garden of Eden in a state of pure innocence. Naked and unashamed, they walked with God, unhindered by guilt, imperfection, or self-consciousness (Genesis 2:25).

In a perfect system, the one that was in place in the Garden of Eden, there was no mention of shame. Adam and Eve lived in pure, unadulterated connection with God. They were naked, yes, but not in a way that induced shame. They were naked in their completeness, bare in their perfection. They were as God created them to be, and in the eyes of this Divine Designer, they were nothing short of perfect. God knew very well that they had no clothes on and that they were naked, but neither Adam nor Eve felt less than because of their weakness.

The narrative takes a pivotal turn in Genesis 3 when Adam and Eve eat from the Tree of the Knowledge of Good and Evil, directly disobeying God's command. This act of disobedience, known as the fall, triggers the immediate awareness of their nakedness and ushers in the unsettling emotion of shame (Genesis 3:7). Sewing fig leaves together for coverings, Adam and Eve attempt to hide their now shameful nakedness from each other. The fig leaves symbolize early efforts to deal with shame through self-made solutions. Humans started a journey of trying to think up solutions for their problems. However, these efforts were futile because they were driven by human effort rather than God's plan.

When God calls out to Adam in the garden, asking, 'Where are you'? (Genesis 3:9 NIV), it's not a question of location but of relationship. Adam responds, 'I heard you in the garden, and I was afraid because I was naked; so I hid' (Genesis 3:10 NIV). The once perfect communion with God had been distorted by fear and hiding, key components of shame.

However, it is crucial to remember the flawless origin of humankind in God's perfect system. We can see our beginnings not as flawed creatures, but as perfectly crafted beings in a perfect system designed to lead us to ultimate perfection. Every time we approach the Throne of Grace, we must remember that we are approaching as beings originally designed for this perfect system. As beings clothed in God's perfect love and His righteousness, shame has no place.

Our deficiencies do not taint us, only our views of ourselves through a lens blurred by the world's standards. However, if we refocus, we can adjust our sight to see ourselves as God sees us: naked, yet perfect. Then we can begin to comprehend our true value in His eyes. Adam needed a wife, and God answered that need, without Adam even asking. You have needs, too. Be assured that God knows them and is eager to fulfil them perfectly, just as He did for Adam.

In the beginning, there was no shame, only perfection. In God's system, we are not defined by our deficiencies but by His perfect design. I want you to remember this as you strive to regain the perfect Eden state of mind in your walk with God. This was the system God set in place for us all along. I want you to embrace your nakedness, your so-called imperfections, as integral parts of your journey to ultimate perfection under God's perfect system.

Shame has caused a breach in relationship and identity. The subsequent curses pronounced by God upon Adam, Eve, and the serpent reflect the far-reaching consequences of their actions, affecting humans' interactions with the earth, each other, and mortality itself.

God then sought out Adam and Eve, who hid in fear. This reveals the first consequence of sin: separation from God. Adam blamed Eve for his disobedience and Eve blamed the serpent (Satan) for tricking her. Here we see the beginning of a cycle of blame that continues throughout history as people try to justify their actions instead of taking responsibility.

The rest of Genesis 3 details the full consequences of sin: pain in childbirth for women, hard labour for men, and thorns and thistles in the ground. These consequences extended to all generations as sin entered into the human race. Nevertheless, amidst this punishment, there is also a glimmer of hope. God pronounces a curse on the serpent, but also promises that one day the offspring of Eve will crush the head of the serpent.

Shame is often described as an emotion that causes people to want to hide or cover up something about themselves that they deem unacceptable or unworthy. This aligns perfectly with the actions of Adam and Eve in the garden, trying to cover up their nakedness with fig leaves and hiding from God. Shame is a powerful force that can lead to destructive behaviours and thoughts, causing people to distance themselves from others and even from God.

Based on biblical teachings, let me share the subtle and not-so-subtle signs that someone is living out a story constrained by shame. Recognizing these signs is the first step in breaking free from shame by the grace of God and stepping out in courage and freedom.

1. AVERSION TO COMMUNION AND FELLOWSHIP

> But if we walk in the light, as he is in the light, we have
> fellowship with one another. (1 John 1:7 NIV)

Maria attends Sunday service but dashes out of church the minute the
service concludes. When members of the congregation try to engage her
in conversation or invite her to join a group, she is overcome by a sense of
unworthiness and shame for feeling like she doesn't quite 'fit in'. Maria's
actions are ruled by her internal struggle, leading her to miss chances for
spiritual growth and community connection.

2. FEAR OF EXPOSURE

> Adam and his wife were both naked, and they felt no
> shame. (Genesis 2:25 NIV)

Tom has kept a diary for years; it is his private sanctuary. One day, he
discovers his diary left open on the kitchen table and learns that his
otherwise supportive roommate read it, unintentionally exposing his fears
and secrets. Feeling his privacy invaded, he battles with the shame of his
secret thoughts being known, hindering his trust in others.

3. SELF-CRITICAL SPEECH AND NEGATIVE SELF-IMAGE

> Therefore, there is now no condemnation for those who
> are in Christ Jesus. (Romans 8:1 NIV)

Alex is on a first date and feels awkward, believing that she is not making
a good impression. When a joke doesn't land, Alex quickly retorts, 'Story
of my life. I'm just boring, I guess'. The date ends, and Alex ruminates over
every word, concluding, 'I'm not likable. Why would anyone be interested
in me'?

4. OVERCOMING MISTAKES BECOMES CHALLENGING

> For all have sinned and fall short of the glory of God.
> (Romans 3:23 NIV)

Elena's fingers hovered above her keyboard, frozen by what she had just realized. In her haste, she had sent a confidential client proposal to the wrong email list. Panic set in as she tried to recall the email, but the damage was done. The spirit of shame was suffocating, paralyzing her from drafting an apology or a solution. She sat, overcome by the enormity of her mistake.

5. Reluctance to Accept Forgiveness

> If we confess our sins, he is faithful and just and will
> forgive us our sins and purify us from all unrighteousness.
> (1 John 1:9 NIV)

Jordan sat in the dim light of the office well after hours, staring blankly at the corrected report on the screen. The numbers now aligned perfectly, but they seemed to mock Jordan's oversight. With everyone having gone home, the silence around was almost palpable.

It had been just a mistake; one incorrect version was uploaded into the report that everyone had missed. However, as the team lead, Jordan felt the weight of the error keenly. The client, although initially upset, had graciously accepted the team's apology and the promise to rectify the oversight immediately.

'You are only human', the client had said, smiling tepidly across the conference table.

The team had echoed this sentiment, understanding that it was an uncommon slip for their usually meticulous leader. 'It happens to the best of us', they'd assured him, clapping Jordan on the back. Instead of comfort, each word seemed to sting, a reminder that Jordan had not lived up to his own standards.

Alone with the hum of the computer, Jordan's thoughts spiralled. The client's forgiveness and the team's supportive words were like Band-Aids offered to a wound Jordan believed didn't deserve to heal. The shame was a heavy cloak, a barrier against the warmth of their forgiveness.

Turning off the monitor, Jordan took a deep breath. 'Accept forgiveness', a quiet voice inside whispered. How could Jordan forgive himself? It seemed a mountain too steep to scale.

6. Persistent Feelings of Guilt and Worthlessness

> There is therefore now no condemnation for those who
> are in Christ Jesus. (Romans 8:1 ESV)

Kevin was a single father working two jobs to provide for his son. However, balancing work and parenting meant that sometimes he couldn't make it to his son's soccer games or school events. This led to a deep-rooted sense of guilt, and a feeling like he was failing as a parent. This spirit of shame stifled Kevin, and he started to believe that his son would resent him. His performance at work suffered, as he was clouded by the persistent feelings of not being enough.

7. Social Withdrawal and Isolation

> The Lord God said, 'It is not good for the man to be
> alone'. (Genesis 2:18 NIV)

Anna has always felt a bit different from her group of friends, not quite fitting the mould of their cool and confident circle. At a vibrant house party, with laughter echoing and glasses clinking, she finds herself shrinking into the background. A comment on her dress, meant as a jest by a friend, feels more like an affirmation of her deepest insecurities. The spirit of shame wraps around her like a cloak, whispering falsehoods into her ear, compelling her to slip out unnoticed, missing out on what could have been a night of cherished memories.

Physical Symptoms of Shame

Shame can affect not just our mental and emotional health but also can manifest physically. The Bible speaks about shame and its repercussions on the human body and soul. In this section, I will highlight some of the physical symptoms for a person living in shame. Recognizing these physical symptoms is a crucial step in navigating through difficulties and finding your path to perfect peace.

- **Altered Body Language**
  Proverbs 14:3 speaks about the folly of pride, which can be related to the feeling of shame when one is prideful and his or her pride is

exposed. The shame he or she feels will often lead to a noticeable change in body language. The person may slouch, avoid eye contact, or exhibit a closed-off posture, as if trying to hide from view.

- **Loss of Strength**
  Psalm 31:10 references the exhaustion and weakening of one's body due to grief and sin. Shame can result in a perceived loss of strength and vitality. Sufferers might feel unusually fatigued, weakened, or generally depleted of energy.

- **Insomnia**
  In Daniel 6:18, King Darius spends a night without sleep amid grave anxiety over Daniel in the lions' den. Shame can cause disruptions in sleeping patterns, similar to anxiety. If you carry shame, you might find it difficult to fall asleep or stay asleep, which can lead to further physical issues.

- **Changes in Eating Habits**
  Proverbs 13:25 speaks about the righteous eating to their hearts' content, but shame can lead to loss of appetite or conversely, to overeating as a way of coping. The guilt and embarrassment that come with shame can severely disrupt normal eating habits.

- **Psychosomatic Symptoms**
  Biblical characters often displayed physical reactions to emotional states. For example, in Genesis 42, when Joseph's brothers experienced guilt, they discussed among themselves how their misdeeds had caused stress. This could be viewed as a recognition of psychosomatic symptoms—when emotional pain causes physical symptoms such as headaches, stomachaches, or even heart palpitations.

- **Aged Appearance**
  Proverbs 12:4 (NIV) talks about a 'wife of noble character' being her husband's crown, but a disgraceful wife is like decay in his bones. Shame not only feels heavy on the mind but can also affect

the physical self, potentially causing one to appear more aged or worn down due to the ongoing stress and negative self-perception it induces.

BREAKING FREE FROM THE GRIP OF SHAME

The Bible offers a path away from shame, emphasizing God's grace and forgiveness. Here are biblical responses to dealing with shame.

1. **Confession and Repentance**
   James 5:16 encourages confession of sins to one another to be healed. The first step in dealing with shame biblically is to acknowledge your sins before God and to repent.

2. **Seeking God's Truth**
   John 8:32 (NIV) states that 'the truth will set you free'. By understanding God's teachings, people can find freedom from the bondage of shame, aligning their worth with how God sees them rather than how they see themselves.

3. **Acceptance of God's Forgiveness**
   First John 1:9 declares that God is faithful and just to forgive sins if we confess them. Accepting this forgiveness is pivotal in releasing the grip of shame.

4. **Transformation through God's Word**
   Romans 12:2 advises against conformity to the patterns of this world and instead calls for renewal of the mind, which comes through immersing oneself in the Word of God. This transformation allows you to live beyond the confines of shame.

Remember, God's vision for humanity is one of freedom and joy, far removed from the binds of shame. 'Therefore, there is now no condemnation for those who are in Christ Jesus' (Romans 8:1 NIV).

In closing off this chapter, we see that from the book of Genesis, two major issues arose.

1. **Fear:** When God called for Adam and Eve, fear gripped them. Adam explicitly stated in Genesis 3:10 (NIV), 'I was afraid because I was naked; so I hid'.
2. **Shame:** A sense of embarrassment and humiliation is evident through their immediate need to cover up their nakedness.

The consequences of their actions introduce mortal vulnerability, including the painful realities of life outside paradise, and death itself. The narrative demonstrates that with the fall came a consciousness of one's limitations and inadequacies, incarnated in these potent emotions of fear and shame.

Remember, recognizing these signs is the first step toward healing and seeking God's truth about identity and worth, which are firmly grounded in His Word and in His Promises.

Now that we have delved into the Word of God, grasping the profound meaning of true freedom and understanding the root cause of our constraints, it's time to shift gears.

The beautiful journey doesn't end here.

Think about this. How much freedom do we really possess if we are perpetually anxious, disheartened, and overwhelmed whenever life throws a curveball at us? Isn't it fair to say that to fully experience freedom, we must have peace that surpasses all understanding, even amidst life's turbulence?

As we sail into the next chapter, we're going to navigate the pathways to perfect peace. This peace will unlock the gates to your ultimate freedom and empower you to not just weather but thrive in life's storms. Remember, our ultimate destination is a life of perfect liberty in Christ. Once you have grasped the concept of how to live in perfect peace, we will then revisit the perfect law of liberty and allow the transformative power of the Holy Spirit to truly free you.

This isn't just about breaking new ground; it's a journey of discovering who God is. By discovering God, you arrive at self-discovery and enlightenment that reaches deep into your soul.

CHAPTER 6

SIGHS OF THE SOUL

Exploring Spiritual Exhaustion

My soul melteth for heaviness: strengthen
thou me according unto thy word.
—Psalms 119:28 (KJV)

UNDERSTANDING WEARINESS OF THE SOUL

Have you ever felt completely drained, not just in body, but in spirit and
mind as well? We all have those moments when the fast pace of life or
the endless demands of work and family leave us feeling exhausted on a
deeper level. It's a feeling that goes beyond physical tiredness, settling into
a weariness that seems to touch our very souls.

Perhaps you've been there, patiently working toward your dreams,
pouring in all your energy, yet seeing no change or progress. It can feel
like an uphill battle, can't it?

The Bible speaks to this state of weariness. In Galatians 6:9 (NIV),
there's a call to 'not grow weary in doing good', even when faced with
obstacles. This isn't just about physical persistence, but about holding onto
faith and maintaining our moral compasses even when the going gets tough.

You see, our journey through life often leads to this profound weariness.
The weight of our missteps, the challenges we face, and the constant
vigilance against negativity can take their toll on us.

These are the burdens that cause our souls to tire: the burdens of iniquity and trials, and the thief who seeks to rob us of our joy and peace.

However, in recognizing and acknowledging these sources of our weariness, we will discover that there is a way out. We will be in a position to face it head-on and look for pathways to the restoration of our souls.

I would like to look at these three causes of weariness individually.

1. THE BURDEN OF INIQUITY

The heavy mantle of iniquity is often carried silently, draped over shoulders with the weight of unseen wrongs. It's a term that threads together secrecy and sin. It is a line drawn through generations, marking the deeds left uncorrected, the choices eschewing redemption. To grasp its meaning and consequence is to recognize a force that influences far beyond you, casting long shadows into the societal fabric itself.

In the dim light of understanding, we often gaze upon our lives and ponder the recurring troubles that beset us. The tangles of sin that bind us—not just mere sins, but the profound and lingering sort, known to many as iniquity—riddle our paths with stumbling blocks. Unlike simple errors or lapses in judgement, iniquity whispers of deeper-rooted issues, patterns of impropriety firmly entrenched in the soil of our hearts.

Have you felt this burden? It is a chain of strongholds woven by hands not entirely your own, yet firmly attached to your being. If so, you are not alone in this sentiment. Iniquity, as chronicled in the sacred texts, is more than sin; it is the deliberate and sustained distortion of righteousness. It's what taints the soul through its obstinate presence, leading many into a labyrinth of despair.

Reflect on the stories of the people of old, and narratives where the consequences of one's errors and wrongdoing spill over into the lives of the descendants. One example is Exodus 20:5–6 (NIV): "'I, the Lord your God, am a jealous God, punishing the children for the sin of the fathers to the third and fourth generation of those who hate me'". It is evident that the impact of one's sins isn't limited to just the individual. It extends through generations within families and communities. Sin has a way of leaving a legacy of harm and persistent struggle, a legacy that should be broken by the blood of Jesus, but is often inherited instead.

Growing up amidst the shadow of alcoholism is like living with a relentless storm hovering above. My family's history was marked not by the milestones of achievements (though they were many), but by the pervasiveness of a single vice: alcohol. It wove its way through the tapestry of our lineage, a dark and tenacious thread binding one generation to the next.

My grandfather, with his boisterous laughter that filled the room, enjoyed the bottle. This charisma, dulled and slurred by the effects of his indulgence, became a source of pain, a legacy he unknowingly passed down. My father, despite his strong work ethic, loyalty, fairness, commitment to all of us, and love for his family, couldn't help but walk in similar footsteps. By God's grace, his drinking did not destroy our family, and for over twenty-three years, he has not touched the bottle.

Why did this cycle of alcoholism course so resiliently through our family tree? Was it a mere coincidence or something bound by a deeper, more ancient tie?

In the process of seeking answers, I turned to something that had long been a pillar in our home: the Bible. Generational iniquity, as chronicled in scripture, speaks of the sins of the fathers visited upon the sons, to the third and fourth generation (Exodus 20:5–6 and Numbers 14:18 NIV). This concept of sin and its consequences flowing through generations opened my eyes to the cycle's stronghold in my family. These spiritual altars were set not in stone but in behaviour, in habit, and in altered mindsets steeped in the comforts and forgetfulness of spirits.

To break free from this cycle, it wasn't enough to recognize the physical manifestations of addiction. It required confronting these generational altars, understanding the spiritual battles at hand, and taking on the full armour of God as described in Ephesians 6:10–18. Within this armour lies the promise of renewal, the power to stand against the wiles of drunkenness and its bondage.

The story of my family, like so many others plagued by addiction, isn't one of sheer will over vice or even about genetics. It is a testament to the deep-rooted, unseen forces that govern habit and hindrance, and the divine strength summoned to overcome them.

I can't claim mine is a family entirely redeemed from this curse. However, I stand as a testament to the possibility of liberation. Armed with this understanding and my faith, I've broken away from the lineage of addiction, piecing together a more sober narrative for future generations.

In this cycle unravelled, there lies hope that each of us can redefine the legacy we leave behind. It is a hope rooted not in erasing the past but in understanding and overcoming it, ensuring that the storm of generational addiction finally dissipates, leaving behind skies clear and futures bright.

The cycle has to end somewhere. I found purpose in the resolve that it ends with me. Breaking a cycle is never an individual pursuit. It's a concerted effort that requires understanding, support, and unrelenting dedication. This is the message I wish to impart—a message of resilience, hope, and the opportunity for redemption that lies within all of us.

When iniquity festers, it does so quietly, subtly, eating away at the fabric of our existence. In the shadows of our worst selves, it conceals itself, be it in unfaithfulness, dishonest gain, or the harbouring of resentment. It's the repeat offender in our moral tapestry, leading us astray time and again.

Yet, iniquity's hold is not an unassailable force. It's a challenge steeped in darkness that yet calls forth light. The pages of scripture unfold tales of redemption, highlighting that the stain of sin can be lifted. Take Ruth, for instance, her life unravelling like a tapestry of grace against a backdrop of generational iniquity. Through her unwavering devotion and love, she emerged as a progenitor of renewal, an emblem of God's restorative power.

This resolve to confront the ensnaring grip of past wrongs brings us to a pivotal juncture. It demands introspection and a fulcrum of change leveraged in repentance. It requires of us more than acknowledging our ancestors' trespasses; it asks for active, conscious realignment to Divine precepts.

It's about choosing a path paved by truth, and thereby constructing bridges where walls once segmented us. It's seeking forgiveness, not as a mere gesture, but as a formidable act of transformation, demolishing the citadels of iniquity that cast long shadows across the lands of our lineages.

Now, you stand upon the precipice of choice. Will you continue to wear the shackles inherited from those who walked before you? Alternatively, shall you pursue liberation for yourselves and generations to follow? Your actions are echoes through time, fortifying foundations or fracturing futures.

We are each called to be architects of a reality that aligns with the ethos of God—one of healing, reconciliation, and equity. Let this be our collective endeavour: to earnestly seek wisdom in identifying the knots of sin and diligently strive to untangle them. In the whisper of your quiet moments, may you entreat the Lord to reveal the hidden fractures within, to shine His light upon the shadows of your iniquity, and to grant you the courage to sever the bonds that hold you captive.

Take a moment to reflect in work and in prayer. What inherited iniquities may be lurking in the corners of your life? What patterns of behaviour have persisted, unchallenged and unchanged? It is time to bring these before the Throne of Grace, to ask for discernment and strength in breaking free from the chains of the past. Seek His guidance, and may your steps henceforth be steadfast upon the path of righteousness, setting forth a heritage not burdened by iniquity, but buoyed by virtue.

2. TRIALS

In the very fabric of our lives, trials are interwoven like threads that often seem to disrupt the harmony of our existence. The Bible speaks of such times, painting them not as punitive measures but as refining moments meant to draw us closer to a Divine purpose. Yet, acknowledging the purpose does not eradicate the weariness. They coexist, the weight of our struggles coupled with the promise of peace in Christ.

Life, in its unpredictability, throws curveballs that inevitably strike us, leaving us to grapple with the impact. We each face our Goliaths, our Red Seas, and our solitary walks through the shadowed valleys. These are the moments that challenge the soul, wrenching from us every semblance of control, until we're left feeling weary and devoid of the peace Christ offers.

Reflect upon a time in life when the hardships felt relentless, when every day was a battle, every night a desperate prayer for relief. For some of you, this might not be a memory but a present reality—an ongoing storm that threatens to consume all your remaining strength. It's in these trenches of life, amidst the mud and the blood, that your resilience is both tested and fortified.

Picture life as a canvas, each trial a brushstroke that at first seems to mar the beauty of the whole picture. It is exhausting to continuously uphold the shield of faith while wrestling with the question that plagues so many believers' hearts: has God forgotten about me?

In such challenging times, the words of Matthew 11:28 (KJV) will serve as a lifeline: "'Come to me, all ye that labour and are heavy laden, and I will give you rest'". Rest—such a simple word, yet it carries within it the promise of refreshment, renewal, and restoration from that profound sense of overwhelming fatigue.

Throughout this arduous ordeal, joy and growth can still bloom. Tribulations are not merciless; they are perhaps the most rigorous instructors of faith and character we'll encounter. Like gold tried in fire, we are refined and purified through our suffering, emerging more resilient and precious (Job 23:10).

It is essential, then, to turn to the One who can replenish an exhausted spirit.

My own reflection takes me back to a time when life felt like a series of skirmishes where defeat seemed inevitable, and God's silence echoed louder than any reassurance.

The day I was fired, the skies over Nairobi mirrored my turmoil. Clouds gathered like an omen, darkening as my resolve was put to the ultimate test. My principles, the core of who I was, had come into conflict with a corrupt request at work. 'Compromise', they said, but the very fibres of my being recoiled. I stood firm, and with that decision, I was cast out, jobless, into the uncertainty of city life.

The aftermath was a sequence out of every person's nightmare. My once-stable world disintegrated. Life seemed to conspire against me; every corner I turned, every effort I made just collapsed into more chaos, more disheartening silence. Nairobi, once a city of dreams, became a landscape where hope wilted beneath a relentless sun.

I sought refuge in churches, their steeples piercing Nairobi's skyline like fingers reaching for divine intervention. There I prayed fervently, exhaustively—a soul pouring out its pain to anyone who would listen. How heavy the silence can weigh upon a weary heart.

Interviews came and went, each one a beacon of hope extinguished upon leaving the room. The void of rejection grew vast and all-consuming. Mechanically, I extended my hand, smiled, and sold the best version of myself, but it was always met with a vacant gaze and a future promise that never materialized.

Nairobi's streets became my traverse, each step a search for something lost. Sometimes, my strength was only a whisper, a thin thread wavering in the wind of my soul's tempest. I cried, and at times, those tears were all I had—a cleansing torrent for a spirit caked in the dust of trials. Each night, as I lay in my bed staring at the ceiling, I felt the intimacy of my faith being stretched to its limits. Even the steadfastness of Mount Kenya seemed easier to move than the mountains of adversity before me.

The adage that 'the night is darkest just before dawn' is more than a platitude; it is a profound truth I lived. Resigned to my fate, contemplating a future where hope was a frail memory, my phone rang. It was an opportunity—not the first, but something in the timbre of the call hinted it might be the last.

The interview was nothing remarkable, but the outcome would be a turning point. They offered me the job, a lifeline thrown to a drowning woman. It was the spark in a smother of darkness, a gate opening to paths abandoned and dreams rejuvenated.

Yet, despite this reprieve, my spirit lagged. Success without internal peace felt hollow. I was a woman saved from drowning yet still too weary to stand. I yearned not just for livelihood, but also for the revival of my essence.

In the wake of my tribulation, it was the balm of Gilead that I sought—a touch from the Lord to restore the vitality of my soul. Jobs are transient, human approval is fleeting, but the serenity bestowed from divine communion is the wellspring of eternal rejuvenation.

Nairobi, with its chaos and beauty, continued. For me, the real work had just begun. I had an inner sanctum to rebuild and a communion with God to renew. It wasn't the streets of the city that would dictate my destiny; it was the quiet, inner conversation, the one that humbles kings and elevates the downtrodden.

In the end, I emerged not just employed but transformed in an oasis found amidst deserts, strength reclaimed in surrender, and faith deepened through despair. This was my story, a short chronicle of a soul reborn.

The trials and scars that mark us are not signs of forsaken souls but of testimony in progress. We do not make this pilgrimage alone; the God of all comfort accompanies us, offering His peace as a sanctuary for the weary.

In this moment of quiet reflection, I invite you to engage with the Author of peace. Expose your heart's scars to Him. Seek His refreshing touch upon your life. Reach out for the peace that surpasses all understanding—a divine peace that reaffirms our strength and resolve.

In this renewed state, you will be equipped to receive all that the Lord has in store for you beyond the trials, beyond the weariness. It is a future crafted by the One who promises never to leave or forsake us.

I would like to caution you, however, not to underestimate the marks that Satan leaves in your mind when it seems like your prayer is unanswered. This is during the times of trial.

3. THE THIEF

The Bible teaches that the devil comes to steal, kill, and destroy. From the early pages of Genesis to the final chapters of Revelation, the story remains the same.

Imagine a smooth operator, a stealthy bandit, or a cunning pickpocket prowling the streets of a bustling city like Nairobi. This person is so skilled in the art of thievery that his exploits are nearly undetectable. He can slip his hands into your pockets, swipe what he wants, and vanish into thin air before you even realize you've been robbed.

Jesus Christ uses this depiction to warn us about the devil's crafty ways of infiltrating our lives. The thief doesn't swoop in with grand gestures and loud bangs. He is subtle, methodical, and insidious. He knows that if his actions were transparent, they would be instantly recognized and thwarted. Therefore, the devil, just like this skilled pickpocket, operates covertly. He works behind the scenes, using our own weaknesses and desires against us.

However, unlike a mere mortal thief, the devil has an arsenal of tactics at his disposal. He knows how to manipulate your thoughts and emotions, fuelling doubt, fear, and temptation within you. He twists the truth and distorts reality to make his schemes seem appealing and desirable. Just like that sneaky bandit who strikes when you least expect it, the devil also knows when to strike: in moments of vulnerability or weakness.

He is driven by an uncontrollable urge to steal. His focus isn't on tangible possessions, though he steals these as well, but rather on the intangible aspects of life: your peace, joy, and faith. He works tirelessly to plant seeds of doubt and despair in your mind until he successfully robs you of these priceless treasures.

However, the devil's tactics don't stop with theft. If he can't steal from you, he will cunningly motivate you to sacrifice your precious possessions and relationships. He is driven by jealousy and envy, and cannot stand to see you blessed. He might stress you, push you to strain your relationships, and rob you of your peace and joy under the guise of pursuing success. He is a master of the art of projecting an aura of happiness and satisfaction, all while quietly sapping your energy.

If his thieving and manipulating tactics aren't effective, the devil turns to destruction. He works tirelessly to ruin your relationships, your health, your mental well-being, and even your faith in God. He isolates you, plants doubts about the support and love of those around you, and then strikes when you are the most vulnerable. Indulging in this destructive behaviour requires no rational justification for the devil. He hates seeing anything good in your life. It's crucial to remember that he doesn't need you to have committed a sin to attack you. All he requires is a loophole, like fear or isolation, to infiltrate your life and wreak havoc.

The Apostle Paul once warned the Ephesians not to give the devil a foothold. Every morning, you need to ensure that your life is aligned with God's principles. Even if the devil is lurking outside your door, roaring like a lion, you should not pay him any attention, especially if he has nothing to take from you.

The devil, much like a thief, never announces his arrival. He is always lurking, ready to strike when you least expect it. You need to stay vigilant, being aware of his scheming tactics. He often comes disguised as something alluring, but in reality, it's nothing more than a trap designed for your destruction.

As followers of Jesus Christ, you must remain steadfast in your faith, never wavering in the face of adversity. By strengthening your belief and surrounding yourselves with godly influences, you can overcome the attacks of the enemy. Remember, the devil loves isolation, so always stay connected with your faith and community. It's your strongest defence against his deceitful attacks!

CHAPTER 7

PSALM 23 AS BEDROCK

Discovering an Unwavering Anchor

The Lord is my shepherd; I shall not want.
—Psalms 23:1 (KJV)

In the tranquil pastures of the human heart, there lies a text that has soothed souls for centuries: Psalm 23, a psalm of David. A sacred composition that has offered solace and strength to countless believers, its verses are a balm for the weary and a banner for the faithful. This book is an invitation to those who seek serenity and yearn for a peace that transcends human understanding. It beckons all of us to rest in the comforting assurance of the Shepherd's care.

This revered psalm is more than just a litany of verses recited in your Sunday schools and by your firesides. It is the voice of King David himself, whispering to you from a place of perfect peace. It's a peace some of you might not truly comprehend. You may have treated it as mere words to help you through your difficult times but you may not have truly embraced their deeper meaning.

How often have we recited Psalm 23 without really understanding its powerful message? Let me share my personal story with you. I remember a time in my life when it felt like every worst-case scenario had come true. During a family holiday in Nanyuki, visiting a tranquil Catholic retreat centre, I found myself reciting Psalm 23. I was in the valley of the shadow of death, both physically and metaphorically, and tears welled up in my eyes. I was repeating these hallowed verses not out of understanding, but out of desperation, hoping that the words alone would pull me out of the situations I felt trapped in. I wasn't resting in the Shepherd's care; I was frantically trying to save myself.

Perhaps my story resonates with you. Perhaps you too find yourself echoing these words because you fear you'll crumble without them. Take heart: there is no shame in admitting this.

Let's take this opportunity to delve deeper into what King David was truly communicating. Let's strive to comprehend the profound essence of Psalm 23, as it forms the bedrock of a soul that has reached the pinnacle of perfect peace. This is the destination we all yearn to arrive at.

Join me on this journey, as we discover the profound tranquillity and sublime serenity that this treasured psalm can lead us to.

STANDING FIRM ON PSALM 23

Psalm 23:1 invites us to consider the areas in our lives where we might feel deficient and to reassess them in the light of faith. It reassures us that in the care of Christ the Shepherd, we can experience an abundance that fills not only our physical needs but enriches our souls as well.

It's a call to rest in the knowledge that with Christ, our needs are understood and attended to, even those we have yet to recognize. Psalm 23:1 is a reflection of trust, an invitation to recognize that true satisfaction and security lie not in earthly riches or accomplishments, but in the shepherdship of Christ, who offers a peace and provision that transcends the ordinary realm of want and need.

First, envisioning the Lord as a shepherd invokes imagery of tender care, guidance, and protection. In ancient times, the shepherd's role was multifaceted: he led his flock to green pastures, sourced calm waters, protected against predators, and retrieved any sheep that lost its way. David, as a shepherd himself before ascending the throne, deeply understood these responsibilities.

The key message of Psalm 23 is foundational to the Christian faith. When you trust in Jesus, an all-sufficient shepherd, He fulfils your needs just as a shepherd adeptly cares for his flock. This does not speak solely of material wants but encompasses spiritual, emotional, and physical needs.

Christ's provision is comprehensive and all encompassing, reaching beyond mere sustenance to the richness of a fulfilled life under His watchful care.

To 'not want' is to be content and provided for, lacking nothing essential. When trust is placed in Christ, an intrinsic sense of peace and contentment arises. It is knowing that regardless of life's fluctuating circumstances, your most profound needs are met in Him. It is not a promise of an easy life devoid of hardship, but rather the assurance that, even amid difficulty, there is sufficiency and hope.

This concept also touches on the nature of desires and the human tendency to want more. Here, the psalm invites you to reevaluate your understanding of what you genuinely need versus what you eagerly want. The discernment to know that what Christ provides is sufficient for your well-being is a sign of spiritual maturity and faith.

When David speaks of walking through the valley of the shadow of death, there is an echo of inevitable challenges yet, simultaneously, an affirmation of trust in Jesus's accompaniment. Faith in Christ yields courage and confidence even as you pass through dark and uncertain seasons. The 'valley' represents life's lowest points, and the comfort found in Jesus's presence is the guiding light that leads you through to greener pastures and still waters.

Psalm 23 further unfolds with the promise of honour and abundance. Jesus sets a table before you in the presence of your adversaries. There is a declaration here of divine honour and provision, an assurance of God's favour even amidst opposition. This speaks to you, the Christian, being blessed and sustained by a source that transcends earthly conflicts. It points to a level of divine intervention and care that rivals all Satan's claims.

Finally, the psalm concludes with a resolute statement of eternal care that follows from a life lived in trust in Jesus. 'Surely goodness and mercy shall follow me all the days of my life' (Psalm 23:6 KJV) is not a passive hope but a certain future for those who follow the Good Shepherd. It's an invitation to a lifelong relationship, with the ultimate promise of dwelling in the house of the Lord forever. It provides a glimpse into eternity that anchors the believer's present reality.

Friends, at its core, Psalm 23 is a contemplative passage that reassures the soul of God's endless provision and care when trust is placed in Jesus. This key insight reminds us that earthly wants and fears fade in the face of divine sufficiency, which provides a path through the wilderness, nourishment among adversaries, and faithful companionship through every season of life. Every verse of this psalm echoes the assurance that with Jesus as your shepherd, you truly lack nothing.

My prayer is that this short study of Psalm 23 will enrich your faith, bring tranquillity to your spirit, and guide you into the divine peace found only in the presence of our Good Shepherd.

CHAPTER 8

THE CORNERSTONE OF THE SOUL

Cultivating Trust

You will keep in perfect peace those whose minds
are steadfast because they trust in you.
—Isaiah 26:3 (NIV)

In chapter 2, we talked about Adam and Eve and the fall of humankind. We came to the understanding that humans were created with a deficiency, which to God was perfect. Adam and Eve were naked, which signified an imperfection or weakness, but this did not change God's view of them. We also saw that Adam had no needs because God knew what Adam needed even before he needed it. In Genesis 2, God saw that Adam needed a wife. Adam was not even aware that he needed a wife. This tells us that God already knows what you need even before you ask Him.

Let us pick up from there. We see that the first time a human was involved in a task was when God created the animals, looked to Adam, and told him to name them. Whatever Adam named them, that is what they were. God said it was good. This shows us that God's intention for humans to think as He does had been accomplished. These names existed in God before the animals came to Adam. Adam, therefore, did not need to create names for animals; he sourced for the names of the animals inside

God. God was therefore the hardware or the hard drive for Adam. It was sufficient for Adam that God knew. A human made in the image of God fears no unknown. The only unknown is what God does not know and there is nothing that God does not know.

Even though the information is not currently active in me, as surely as it is active in God, I have it.

When you understand this, you will then possess the comfort of the Holy Spirit. He is called the advocate. John 14:16–17 (NLT) states,

> And I will ask the Father, and he will give you another Advocate, who will never leave you. He is the Holy Spirit, who leads into all truth. The world cannot receive him, because it isn't looking for him and doesn't recognize him. But you know him, because he lives with you now and later will be in you.

This means that if anything demands remembrance, the Holy Spirit will bring remembrance at the same moment. In John 14:27 (KJV), the Lord said the following words: "'Peace I leave with you, My peace I give to you; not as the world gives do I give to you. Let not your heart be troubled, neither let it be afraid'". This is what Jesus Christ meant: as long as you stand firm with the Holy Spirit by your side, conscious that He is a very present help, then peace will be your portion. You will not need to be afraid. Your mind will be focused on the Holy Spirit because you trust that He is available to you every time you need Him.

My friends, if you can dare to let God think for you and through you, I can assure you that you will live at peace.

Jesus further elaborates in John 15:4–5 on the necessity of an intimate connection with God. He uses the analogy of a vine and branches to emphasize our dependence on Him. The fruitfulness of our lives is contingent upon our ability to remain in Him. Thus, our efforts should be geared toward abiding in His presence and sustaining an unceasing fellowship with Him. Mine is simply to abide. My consciousness of God and my consciousness of Him in me is what I should focus on.

Your labour should be to abide. Remember that your labour is supported by the Holy Spirit, who aids you at all times. When you stand before a circumstance, you must know that you have an answer. If you have a need, you have provision. If you have a question, the Lord will surely answer you. You should constantly tell you soul these words. Remind the devil that all of God's promises are yes and amen. Remind him that Jesus did everything for you. He won the battle and had victory for you because you are His child.

It is important you realise that you have a covenant with God. A covenant is always between two people. Many of the times, we call God a covenant-keeping God but God can only keep a covenant with another person and that person is you. What covenant have you made with God? Your covenant in this instance is that you will abide in Him. Once you make this covenant, make sure you do not betray it. Go ahead—make the covenant with God now. Say to your soul, 'My soul, remember this, when I stand before a circumstance, I will not betray my covenant with God, which it to abide in Him'. You need to be aware that when you betray your covenant with God, God is under no obligation to protect you. However, if you keep your end of the bargain, you can be assured that no devil can oppress you. He will try, but the Lord will protect you.

Your labour is to change the perception in your mind and believe you know the one who has said He will never leave or forsake you. Please, please, digest it and ask the Holy Spirit to give you the grace to believe it. I know it can be hard to believe that you can live life without having to think much or worry about anything as long as you have the Holy Spirit. Believe it, friends. This is very possible.

I will even share with you a personal story so simple it will blow your mind.

One day, I was desperately searching for a single sheet of paper, a precious record of my instructions from God scribbled in ink, which seemed hopelessly lost.

To me, this wasn't just any piece of paper. It was a sacred conversation between me and a higher power, marked by the sincerity of a person in search.

In defeat, I reached out not into the void, but to a familiar, often-ignored presence: the Holy Spirit. This was so wrong as He should have been my first go-to. However, life happened as it did. Softly, I asked for help to recall where I had placed that note.

I left my office, shutting the door behind me, having surrendered the outcome to the Holy Spirit. I knew He would not let me down. He had never let me down before, so why would He do it now?

The following day as I got into the office, the Holy Spirit gently nudged me toward a journal hidden away.

There, I found my answer in a silent victory that doesn't shout but quietly unfolds in the soul. Laughter sprang from me, mixed with divine humour. 'Why do we struggle alone when we have You'? I spoke aloud, rediscovering my misplaced document.

The gentle nudges of the Holy Spirit hold mighty power to calm storms and soothe spirits. This force doesn't force itself upon us but waits quietly for us to reach out. Being conscious of His presence with us all the time allows us to find His help that's vast and unfailingly steadfast.

I share this humble story, an everyday incident touched by wonder, to affirm that you, too, can experience this guiding comfort. Welcome the Holy Spirit at all times. Speak with Him like you would a dear friend. Laugh with Him. His presence is subtle but constant. He is a reliable guide.

However, for you to enjoy His help, you have to be sure that He is in you and that you have been filled with the Holy Ghost. One of the evidences or signs that you are filled with the Holy Ghost is that you are able to speak in heavenly language, that is, speak in unknown tongues.

If you have not received this power, and you want to receive Him, the Governor of the earth, I invite you to extend your own invitation to Him by saying this prayer.

Dear Lord Jesus Christ,

I recognise that I am in need of more of Your power in my life. Your Word promises that when we ask, we receive. You also told me that You would not leave me comfortless. I confess that I cannot make it in this world without your Holy Spirit. Please fill me with your Holy Spirit (with the evidence of speaking in tongues). I am asking this of you by faith right now.

I believe that you have filled me and I receive the infilling of Your Holy Spirit in my heart right now. Thank

you Holy Spirit for being the power at work in my heart
and in my life.

I give you all the praise and all the glory, in Jesus's
name, amen!

Now start to pray and allow the Holy Spirit to speak through you.
Don't be afraid. Just let go and trust.

No matter the size of your challenges, the Holy Spirit is a lifelong
companion, always near and ready to shed light on your path with
wisdom that goes beyond what we can fathom. In life's challenges and
daily vicissitudes, who He is brings forth answers waiting to be grasped,
solutions longing to be unearthed. Just be still, listen closely, and have
faith. Go ahead—try it.

You Will Keep in Perfect Peace in Christ

In today's tumultuous world, the quest for peace can often feel unattainable.
Yet the promise we find in scripture, particularly in Isaiah 26:3 (NIV),
which states. 'You will keep in perfect peace those whose minds are
steadfast, because they trust in you', offers a beacon of hope to those
seeking solace in spiritual truth.

In chapter 2, we discussed that humanity's initial state of exposure
and vulnerability was seen as perfect in the Lord's eyes. Their nakedness,
a symbol of human imperfection, did not alter God's perception of His
creation.

The most profound act of Christ that brought us peace is his
redemption. If you are in Christ, it's important to understand that you're
part of a unique system that guides you in any situation. Within this
system, there's no room for doubt or fear. When you feel something deeply
in your heart, trust it to be true, because you are connected to the source:
Jesus, who provides all you need.

The Bible conveys a clear message about your identity as a child of
God. It tells you that, originally, God did not design you to exert effort
in creating things. It wasn't until after the fall that human effort became
necessary. Prior to this, Adam did not need to use his intellect for creation.
In Genesis 2:21–22, we read,

And the LORD God caused a deep sleep to fall upon Adam, and he slept: and he took one of his ribs, and closed up the flesh instead thereof; And the rib, which the LORD God had taken from man, made he a woman, and brought her unto the man.

While Adam slept, God created Eve, suggesting that the most significant of Adam's 'contributions' came about effortlessly, without any mental exertion on his part. This illustrates that, according to the Bible, humanity's most profound creations are often those that occur without our direct, conscious input.

Sleep, as designed by God, serves as a period of restoration. The divine intent behind sleep is to rejuvenate us fully. In a state of refreshment, aging seems like a distant concept. Our bodies and minds recover, mirroring a practice that God set in motion through the Sabbath. On this day, and in the sabbatical year, fields were left fallow. The land was undisturbed and allowed to rest, signifying a time for renewal. Just as the land, given rest, regains its vitality, we too are reenergized through God's gift of rest and refreshment.

Humans were originally created with the potential for immortality before the fall. Though not immortal, at least for now, humans do experience sleep. The concept of sleep may carry over into the afterlife, as suggested by the biblical account where Adam, who was created to never die, was put into a deep sleep by God.

In an ideal state, sleep is supposed to rejuvenate us fully, leaving us completely revitalized upon waking. However, sometimes we wake up still feeling tired or even with a headache, which marks a discrepancy from this ideal. This indicates that our bodies and souls have not been wholly rested or refreshed. This incomplete rest contributes significantly to the aging process.

Thus, the extent of our bodies' aging correlates with the quality of our sleep. If we're unable to achieve fully restorative sleep on a regular basis, our bodies may feel the effects of weariness more acutely. Consequently, the saying 'you are as old as you feel' might reflect the effects of cumulative fatigue rather than chronological age.

When someone asks your age and you say you're forty, remember that age by itself isn't what's important. Reflect on the words of David in Psalms when he prayed, 'Lord, teach us to number our days that we may gain a heart of wisdom'. David recognized that life is fleeting, typically spanning seventy to eighty years, and often filled with challenges and suffering. In contrast, our ancestors lived for centuries.

Consider this an invitation to rethink your perspective. Seek from God not just years but renewed strength with each passing day. You might doubt, thinking such renewal is beyond reach. Yet, recall Moses, who at 120 had clear vision and abundant energy to traverse the desert.

Believe in the potential for strength in age because Moses's story is a testament to it. Through Christ's redeeming power, you too can showcase this miraculous renewal of strength. May you find that with each night's rest, you awaken with renewed vitality, growing stronger as your years advance.

I've chosen to welcome aging gracefully, as inspired by biblical teachings. The Bible mentions that although Moses had hair as white as snow, his vigour did not fade. Similarly, representations of Jesus portray Him with white hair, symbolizing His eternal nature as the 'Ancient of Days'. Yet, these images do not depict a deity limited by time or weakened with age. In fact, they emphasize God's enduring strength and swiftness, especially when He enacts justice. Therefore, I too believe that being united with Christ promises the potential for enduring vitality.

All I've mentioned indicates that God provides a system of rest and renewal.

CHAPTER 9

A SOUL REJUVENATED

The Art of Divine Restoration

He restoreth my soul: he leadeth me in the paths
of righteousness for his name's sake.
—Psalms 23:3 (KJV)

In the previous chapter, we explored how those who focus their minds on God and trust in Him find themselves enveloped in perfect peace. This divine peace transcends circumstances. It's about your inner state rather than your external environment. You'll recognize that you've embraced this peace when life's upheavals don't disrupt your calm. This constancy of peace is what I refer to as perfect peace. While God can provide peace amid difficulties, His ultimate intention is to lead you to a state of peace that surpasses all understanding, unaffected by life's storms.

Jesus conveyed a profound message in John 14:26–27, telling us not to be weighed down by worry. We are called to trust in God and also in Jesus Himself. This implies that anxiety often stems from a lack of faith. Peace is an option we can freely choose; it's within our grasp and is not restricted by what Christ offers us. I have made a commitment to fully appreciate and utilize the benefits that Jesus's sacrifice secured, but not for comfort's sake. Rather, it's out of honour for His suffering on the cross. Every provision He suffered for, I'm determined to live by but not necessarily enjoy. This leads me to understand that enduring hardship isn't meant to be the norm.

Instead, God uses our tough times as tools to develop character or achieve purposes in us. He doesn't wish for us to suffer endlessly.

Conversely, the enemy wants you to adopt a way of thinking that justifies ongoing struggle, which keeps you trapped far longer than you are meant to be. Therefore, once a difficult season is meant to end, resolve not to linger in it any longer than necessary.

When God is at work within you, shaping you for a particular season, no religious doctrine should detain you beyond His intended timeframe. God's process aims to refine our desires so that they resonate with His divine plan. Once our desires sync with God's intentions, the instant we conceive a thought sets the heavens in motion; the instant we pray for it, it's granted.

It's not about our thoughts compelling God to act; rather, it's our prayers that He responds to. He operates on earth exclusively through our answered prayers. Every occurrence in your life unfolds in response to prayer. My friends, always remember that receiving answers to your prayers paves the way to untold happiness.

My friends, I want you to understand an important truth: often, we harbour hopes and expectations that we have crafted ourselves. When we turn to God with our requests, the typical question that arises is, 'What will I gain from this'? However, it is crucial to recognize that the hopes we generate on our own are not promises from God. Because they are not His promises, God is not obliged to fulfil them. He is committed to fulfilling the expectations that He has set forth for us.

Many times, we face disappointments over things God never assured us of. We envisage a particular outcome, decide on it, and then hold onto a false hope that if God is guiding us, certain things should naturally follow. However, this isn't always true, as shown by the disciples of Jesus. They followed Him, hoping to achieve greatness and authority. Yet, Jesus never promised them such rewards; they had set those expectations for themselves.

The inclination to cling to false hopes isn't eliminated by professing faith in Jesus as Lord and Saviour. This tendency can persist even as one grows deeper in his or her faith. Even prominent figures in the faith may still hold onto personal expectations. For example, someone with deep spiritual insights might wrongly assume that this should automatically lead to a large following.

In essence, discerning the difference between our self-made hopes and God's true promises is vital at every stage of our spiritual journeys.

Many of the disappointments we experience do not stem from unfulfilled divine promises but rather from our own expectations. Take friendships, for instance. You might believe that if your friend Njeri gets a promotion, you should naturally get one too because of your bond. When reality doesn't align with these expectations, it leads to anger and resentment. However, this results not from any promise but from the expectations you've set for yourself.

Be mindful—such reactions reflect the consequences of the fall, eating from the Tree of Knowledge of Good and Evil. When someone close to us progresses, we often subconsciously expect to benefit too, setting us up for emotional hurt that nobody intended.

Remember, true peace comes from maintaining focus on God and trusting in Him. Relying on human aid can be futile, not because people often choose not to help, but because they are often too preoccupied with their own challenges to act.

The ability to remember comes from God, and the butler finally remembered Joseph. It's not that the butler left prison preoccupied with memories of Joseph's kindness. In fact, if you had asked the butler about Joseph right after his release, he would have confidently predicted Joseph's prompt release too, grateful for the aid he had received. The butler might have even staked his life on it. However, as time passed, the butler became caught up in life again and moved ahead.

Here's an important reminder: God did not anchor His promises in other people. He anchored them in Himself. Your hopes should not rest on others; this mindset helps you remain grateful when someone does lend you support. Relying on false hopes can erode your sense of gratitude and weaken your faith. Fix your hope in the truth of God's Word instead. If His promises are found in the scriptures, then they are reliable. If God communicates with you, whether through prayer, worship, dreams, or visions, you can trust in those assurances.

If something is not promised in the Bible and God hasn't personally revealed it to you, tell your soul to be at peace and be still. Elevate God's true promises over any misplaced hope. Reinforce to yourself that what God has pledged is more than enough.

Strive for a place where disappointment doesn't reach and heartache is a stranger. Indeed, such a state is attainable. This is not to suggest I've been immune to pain; undoubtedly, people have let me down, and my heart has felt the repercussions, sometimes even fracturing under the weight. However, life's trials have taught me resilience and instilled wisdom within.

There have been those who've promised to support me, to stand by me and uplift the calling I've felt in my life. They've confidently committed to help in various ways. Yet, when their support was most needed, they turned away, pretending not to understand the gravity of the situation. Experience is a harsh teacher, showing that reliance on others can sometimes lead to disappointment.

This resembles Peter's story with Jesus. Peter's vows of unwavering loyalty and dedication were genuine, but even with the best intentions, he faltered. He wasn't ill-natured, just human.

Often when people judge their own capabilities, they do so without considering what they haven't yet faced. Many are confident of success until they're actually tested. At that point, commitment falters. Former supporters don't want their reputations tarnished. This is mirrored in how some fans profess undying loyalty until some bad press about the person reveals his or her limits.

Isn't this similar to what happens in some marriages? In the honeymoon phase, partners promise the world to each other. Yet, when difficult times arrive, they backpedal, claiming this isn't what they signed up for. During the wedding vows, they pledge to stay together until death. However, when challenges arise, those promises can feel like distant memories.

This is why it's vital to qualify our vows with 'by the Grace of God'. James 4 emphasizes this not as a phrase of doubt, but as one carrying the certainty of divine support. The Bible tells us God's grace is sufficient. When we invoke 'by the Grace of God', we're calling upon a higher power that won't fail us, even when our strength does.

When Peter expressed his affection for Jesus, he received a warning about the devil's desire to sift him. Jesus emphasized that Satan was aware of Peter's weaknesses. Nevertheless, with God's grace, there's always a way out when challenges arise. Jesus reassured Peter that even though things might not be understood then, in time, they would become clear and would be overcome.

It's essential for you to have empathy, knowing that everyone's spiritual journey is different, not because of a lack of faith but because he or she is in a different stage. You should be patient and support your fellow believers, just as Jesus advised Peter to be supportive of the other disciples. Jesus knew Peter would be the first to face tests, and if Peter stumbled, it would signal the significant challenges awaiting the rest.

Often in our spiritual lives, we cling to false hopes not grounded in God's promises. In your faith, you must not take anything for granted. You should patiently await God's revelations and place your confidence only in what He has made known. Presumptive beliefs might motivate you momentarily, but if held too tightly, they can disrupt your spiritual seasons.

Continuing on your journey toward perfect peace, it's important to recognize obstacles that can hinder you. Bearing burdens, like fears, anxiety, and sickness, can prevent you from achieving perfect peace. In Matthew 11:28, Jesus reached out to those overwhelmed by life's struggles and offered them rest, a liberation from these heavy burdens.

What Jesus proposes is a different kind of yoke, one characterized by meekness and lowliness of heart. Carrying this yoke is actually your path to peace. Meekness isn't about weakness; it's about reserving judgement until we hear from God. Consider Moses, highlighted as the meekest man on earth, who consulted with God before making any decisions.

This spirit of meekness and lowliness of heart is vital. It's a warning against self-importance based upon your achievements or status. When you start to believe you are something special because of what you have accomplished, you invite stress into your life and a pressure to continue performing. This performance trap can eat away at your inner peace.

True freedom comes when you can fully surrender yourself so that God may work through you. At this level of trust, it's not about knowing every step ahead but about being confident in God's guidance. Knowledge is indeed valuable, and you must strive to gain it through the Holy Spirit. Yet, when faced with performance demands, your reliance should be on the Spirit to enable you to use what you know or to provide the wisdom you lack.

John 14:26 reminds us that we are not left alone; the Helper is with us. The danger lies in feeling disarmed by your lack of knowledge, thereby rendering yourself, and paradoxically the Helper, powerless.

To simplify, the path to perfect peace involves shedding the heavy loads that fear and worries place upon you. Jesus offers a lighter load, one of gentleness and lowliness in heart, which actually leads you to rest. Your pride and the pressure to perform are obstacles you must overcome. You find freedom in trusting God's voice and allowing the Holy Spirit to equip you for every situation. You don't need to have every answer; you only need to remain open and dependent on the divine guidance at your side.

Remember, you are the most powerful force on earth. On earth, you are stronger than God. That's right. You have more influence on your earthly existence than you might think. Inviting divine intervention into your life and actions is in your hands. What you permit Him to do with your hands and through you, God will do. This doesn't mean you're powerless if you haven't realized this; action is key. You need to put in the effort, study, and prepare. Once you've done everything within your power, stand firm in the belief that you will receive the support you need. Rest assured, knowing that help is on its way.

Jesus told His disciples that even though He would be leaving them, they wouldn't be left alone. He promised to send the Holy Spirit, who would be with them just as Jesus had been. This means the Holy Spirit is as real and present as Jesus was when He walked with His disciples. Jesus even said it was better for Him to go because, unlike Jesus who could only be in one place at a time, the Holy Spirit could be with all of them, all at the same time and all the time. When Jesus was there, He could only talk to one person at a time, but the Holy Spirit can be with all of them, teaching and guiding them simultaneously. This is why Jesus considered the Holy Spirit's coming to be so important. He wanted His followers to understand that with the Holy Spirit, they have a helper always ready to support them. The hardship many Christians face often comes from not fully recognizing or depending on the Holy Spirit's role in their lives.

In those moments when you feel utterly powerless, you essentially limit God's influence in your life. You can realize you've shut Him out by the despair in your actions and the loss of hope in your demeanour. Yet, remember, never lose faith in God for He hasn't lost faith in you. He is capable. This becomes apparent when, in seeking solutions, your heart instinctively turns to Him, knowing all is not lost unless the Holy Spirit deems it so. This trust is what brings true peace.

Jesus's departure was pivotal because He left us the Holy Spirit, who can be everywhere at once, aiding in carrying out the mission He entrusted to His disciples. Sent in different directions, they were never alone. The Holy Spirit's support is never diluted by being shared among many.

Consider this reminder: 'Oh what peace we often forfeit, oh what needless pain we bear, all because we do not carry everything to God in prayer'. It's important to realize that not every challenge is a test from God. Sometimes, it's simply a matter of not recognizing the help that's always there. Ignoring the presence of the Holy Spirit limits His ability to assist. Remember, the Holy Spirit thrives where He is welcomed and invited. Turning to Him with a humble heart is the key.

When you're traveling with a friend and you're both hungry or thirsty, but only your friend has water, it's not the time to start complaining about your thirst. Instead, simply ask your friend if he or she can share some of the water with you. Ignoring that he or she has what you need and not asking for help is both foolish and prideful.

Remember, help isn't just about what you have right now. With the Holy Ghost, you have everything you need and can face any circumstance. To keep your soul consistently refreshed, you should direct any life pressures toward the one who can help you. Keeping your struggles to yourself will only make you feel more helpless. If you don't ask for help, you're also preventing God from being able to assist you. Train your soul to recognize that you're never helpless or without comfort, as the Holy Ghost is always with you. If you don't get into the habit of doing this, your soul will react based on limited understanding, missing out on the support and guidance available to you.

CHAPTER 10

TOWARD THE HORIZON OF LIBERATION

Welcoming True Freedom

In earlier sections, we discussed how, before the fall, humans in their perfect state didn't have the four types of fear that cripple people today.

Let us address each of these fears individually.

1. FEAR OF INSUFFICIENCY

In the beginning, Adam and his wife didn't wear clothes. They were completely naked, and they weren't embarrassed about it. They were in a state of innocence, where doing wrong wasn't a part of their lives, much like how we consider righteousness. Even though they talked and lived without clothes, they never felt exposed or insufficient. Think about it this way: when you're about to change clothes in your room, you probably make sure no one can see you by locking the door. That's because being seen without clothes often makes us feel vulnerable or not enough.

Before the fall changed everything, Adam and his wife didn't feel that way. They didn't see their lack of clothing as a problem because they felt completely accepted by God. Since God didn't focus on their nakedness, they didn't worry about it either. This sense of being accepted as we are can help us overcome feelings of not being enough. God doesn't focus on our flaws, and similarly, we're encouraged to look beyond imperfections in others.

In 2 Corinthians 5:19, the Bible tells us about God's work through Christ to bring everyone back to Him and not focus on their mistakes. This shows that God looks at us through a lens of love and forgiveness and not at our shortcomings.

That's why it's important to be rooted in the light, because once you are, your interaction with darkness will be influenced by the potential of light, not by the damage darkness has caused. When speaking to someone, focus on the potential and hope God sees in him or her not on the negative impact sin has had. If we only focus on the person's past mistakes, we'll end up condemning the person, reminding the person of what he or she already knows: how his or her life has been affected. Instead, God's approach is not to hold anyone's wrongs against him or her. He has given us the mission to bring people back to Him and show them the path of reconciliation.

I want to make it clear that even after Adam and Eve made a mistake, God still approved of them. What changed when they ate the fruit from the Tree of Knowledge was how they saw themselves. How much of who God says you are has changed because of how the world has labelled you? Could you be so afraid of what the world thinks of you that you have been paralysed by its thoughts and completely lost yourself?

God loves you just as you are.

2. THE FEAR OF THE UNKNOWN

God showed Adam the animals to see what names he would give them. We learn in class about something called 'liquidity preference'. It's the fear of the uncertain future that makes people prefer having cash rather than investing in assets. This is often because of speculative motives, which basically means people think having a lot of cash will protect them from problems and offer an escape when things get tough. Have you heard of situations where someone felt called by God to give away all the money in his or her bank account? I've been in that position myself. The lesson behind this dramatic action was to understand that true safety and peace come from trusting in God, not from the amount of money we have. I emptied my entire bank account because God asked me to do so.

Please don't try this at home. It could be very dangerous and is more complicated than it seems. Nonetheless, it's crucial to understand that the idea of giving, in God's view, was always meant to teach us that we should trust in God for our future. This concept applies not just to donating to the church but to all forms of giving. Many of us live below the prosperous life God intended because we hoard what we were meant to use or share. Saving money is smart and I save money, too, but problems arise when we have savings that we feel we cannot use as God directs. This reminds me of the story Jesus told about a rich man in Luke 12:16–21, who had so much harvest he didn't know where to store it. He decided to build bigger barns to keep all his goods, thinking this would secure his future against any problem that could arise. However, this mind-set led him away from relying on God and instead trusting solely in his wealth. Fear of what the future holds can often control us, but God wants us to live joyfully, free from these fears. God showed this when he brought animals to Adam to name, despite Adam's lack of formal education. Adam was able to name them all by drawing knowledge directly from God. Everything Adam named kept its name.

3. THE FEAR OF NEED

Being alone isn't beneficial for anyone. As mentioned before, Adam didn't realize he needed a wife until God pointed it out to him and fulfilled his need, even before he asked. Had Adam been by himself, he might have settled into his life, content with what he had, without realizing what he lacked. He focused only on what he had and never worried about what was missing, which didn't make him feel inferior. Some of you believe that more money will solve your problems, which might be partially true. However, without guidance from Christ, more money could actually lead to more problems. My advice is to appreciate what you have and recognize that you lack nothing. Understand that God has blessed you. Acknowledge that you are complete with Jesus. Without this acknowledgement, no amount of money will truly satisfy you.

Investing your resources with the hope that they will bring true peace to your heart won't bear the fruits of righteousness. The increase in your wealth might temporarily boost your confidence, but this is often based on the false peace the world offers. You might tell yourself that with more money, you could do more good: evangelise more, help more, give more. However, this is a misconception. For instance, if you hear about someone spending four million dollars on medical treatment and realize your savings of 130 million Kenyan shillings only converts to one million dollars, you might start worrying about affording such care for your own family. This fear leads you to envision scenarios that haven't happened. Remember, fear is just another form of faith, but it's not the kind we should strive for.

4. GOD CAUSED A DEEP SLEEP

Building a house or guarding a city without the Lord's guidance is pointless. To truly succeed, we must recognize that continuous effort and vigilance are necessary. If you knew when a thief would come, you'd be ready, but since you don't, staying alert is essential. The Bible teaches that it is vain to wake up early, sleep late, only to reap the bread of sorrow. This is futile. God blesses His beloved with rest. All efforts should start from a place of rest, acknowledging that without God's blessing, our hard work is in vain. By accepting this, we can focus on endeavours that are truly blessed and filled with grace.

Ecclesiastes 10:10 (NIVUK) is a well-known verse from the Bible and often quoted in various contexts. It reads, 'If the axe is dull and its edge unsharpened, more strength is needed, but skill will bring success'. This verse encapsulates the idea that diligence and wisdom are essential for success. This teaches us that using a dull axe requires more effort, while wisdom leads to success. This wisdom is akin to sharpening the axe. In today's world, sharpening the axe could be compared to using a power saw. With a power saw, you don't need special training or great strength to cut down a tree. All that's necessary is to know the right direction to cut so the tree falls safely. While some may prefer the traditional method of using an axe, it often results in physical strain and slow progress. The message here is that adopting modern tools and methods can lead to better outcomes with less effort.

Adam's peace came because he realized he wasn't responsible for anything in his life. Men, especially, don't be overwhelmed by the need to perform. Remember, you're the leader of your home, not the keeper of the entire universe. Being the head of your family doesn't mean you have to shoulder every burden alone. If you lose touch with God, the pressure to succeed can lead you to make choices that bring more stress than grace into your life. This stress wears you down and can unintentionally harm the very family you're trying to support. It leads to unnecessary anger and conflicts, especially with loved ones who've been eagerly waiting for your return. Sometimes, the worry over a single deal can disrupt your inner peace. Remember, true peace doesn't come from worldly successes.

I have come to unplug you from every dimension of thought that has kept you bound to the yoke of fear. Satan has used this yoke of fear to keep you in slavery. The Lord surrounds you with a song of deliverance from your enemies until all your fears are gone.

Jesus Christ was crucified to bring us redemption, so that the blessings promised to Abraham could reach us, the Gentiles, and we could receive the Holy Spirit by faith. This Spirit is our assurance of God's promise. Hebrews 2:14 explains that Christ shared our humanity and died to defeat the devil, who had power over death.

This act wasn't just to sympathize with our struggles. Although Jesus understands our sufferings (He, as our high priest, empathizes with our weaknesses), it is more than that. His death had a purpose beyond companionship in suffering. When He offers consolation or advice during our troubles, we can fully accept it, knowing that Jesus has walked the path before us.

Understand that Jesus didn't come merely to offer sympathy. While His compassion and empathy are initial steps, they lead to a greater goal. If you only accept the comforting aspect of Jesus's role as a priest, then you're just touching the surface of what He offers.

Jesus became human because only beings with physical bodies can experience death. He chose to die to free us from the consequences the curse of breaking God's law. Being hung on a cross was considered such a curse. Galatians 3:13 (KJV) states, 'Cursed is every one that hangeth on a tree'. By willingly facing this cursed death, Jesus offered redemption to us all. This concept is crucial to comprehend as we move forward in understanding.

Jesus Christ took on a curse for us, and the only way He could do this was by having a body capable of death. It's said that a person must be hung on a tree to be cursed, and Jesus did exactly that. However, His death was more than just an endpoint; it was a necessary step to achieve a greater purpose. To truly honour Jesus's sacrifice, we shouldn't just mourn on Easter; instead, we should understand and live by the principles He suffered for. That means to honour His death is not to cry at Easter. To honour His death is to find the reason why He chose that gruesome pathway. After this, you then decide that if Jesus chose that pathway, the only way you can honour Him is to live for everything He paid for. Even if it is not important to you, it is so important to Him that He chose to die.

Jesus's choice to endure such suffering was driven by how crucial these principles were to Him—so significant that He was willing to give His life. Honouring Him means living for the values for which He paid the ultimate price.

Love can bring joy, but it also has its challenges. One common hurdle is when a heartfelt sacrifice isn't valued by the one you love. It's important to respect and appreciate the effort behind a gift, even if it doesn't hold the same meaning to you.

Let me illustrate with a fictitious story, for example. With my husband's birthday approaching, I stumbled upon a stylish shirt perfect for him. Despite planning to use my recent KES 10,000 earnings on myself, his happiness was my priority. I was shocked to learn the shirt cost KES 8,000, but decided my husband deserved the treat.

However, when I presented the shirt, my husband disparagingly dismissed it. Imagine the disappointment! This is reflective of a greater sacrifice, like that of Jesus, who made the ultimate sacrifice with the expectation of reverence, not indifference.

In essence, it's key to honour and cherish the sacrifices made for us, regardless of our personal tastes. When someone gives us a gift, it's a gesture of love deserving gratitude. Sadly, in my story, the shirt eventually found its way to my husband's cousin—a silent testimony to the unappreciated sacrifice.

We often take for granted the great sacrifice Christ made for us, paying for our redemption with His life. Jesus willingly gave up His divine status, choosing not to cling to His equality with God. Instead, He embraced humility, becoming a human like us because of how much the Father loved us. Jesus was saddened by how much the Father was saddened when He looked at us. Because of Jesus's love for the Father, He agreed to die on the cross.

In our daily hustle, driven by personal ambitions, we tend to forget this profound humility and the extent of Jesus's sacrifice. He faced mockery, suffering, and the cross, all so that death and Satan could be destroyed. He deemed the scorn He would face as worth enduring, considering what His death would accomplish.

We must never forget the immense value Jesus saw in sacrificing Himself for us, and we should honour His gift with the reverence it deserves. His sacrifice is too important to be taken for granted. Jesus cannot treat the price as nothing and then have us treat the gift as nothing.

That it was a gift does not mean it was free. Salvation is a gift, but it is the costliest thing paid for in the history of humanity. Amazingly, we value things according to how freely we receive them, not according to the price that the one who made the sacrifice paid.

What I am doing here is first exalting what Christ paid. Once you arrive at understanding what Christ paid for, you will know that you must live your entire life protecting what He paid for. I need your eyes to be open to the reason why fear must never be a part of your life. You must never permit fear to be a part of your life.

When Jesus saw us, He knew we were vulnerable to death because we are made of flesh and blood. He loved us deeply and realized the devil was using our fear of death to oppress us. Every time we felt intimidated, we lived below our potential, which pained Jesus.

Understanding that defeating the devil directly wasn't the solution, Jesus chose to become human and to share in our experiences. By allowing the devil to take hold of him, Jesus took on our suffering. This way, when we are afraid or crying, Jesus comprehensively understands our pain.

However, Jesus's plan went further than just empathy. To challenge the devil's hold over us, He had to face him directly. Jesus's strategy involved a sacrifice; by facing the devil himself and taking our place, Jesus could shield us from it. While enduring this ordeal, Jesus acted as a barrier between us and the devil. The death we were destined for, he faced for us.

While it seemed that Jesus was merely suffering, he was, in fact, seeking a way to overcome the devil entirely. Through his sacrifice, Jesus not only empathized with our struggles but actively worked to free us from the devil's grip once and for all. Jesus was looking for access to Satan so that He could destroy Satan completely.

CHAPTER 11

VICTORY OVER DEATH'S SHADOW

Claiming Eternal Triumph

Since the children have flesh and blood, he too shared in
their humanity so that by his death he might destroy him
who holds the power of death—that is, the devil.
—Hebrews 2:14 (NIV)

In the previous chapter, we discussed how Christ's sacrifice paid the price
for our freedom. This chapter's key message is that you can defeat the devil
and overcome evil by realizing that Jesus's death already broke the power of
death. Understanding the true meaning behind the crucifixion empowers
you to believe that evil has no control over you. In essence, *the devil does
not exist!* This idea highlights that our lack of awareness of Satan's defeat
at the cross gives Satan and death their power. Jesus's death overcame the
one ruling over death. Now, when evil attempts to affect you, it's like a
powerless thief acting without any real power. This connects to our earlier
conversation in chapter 3 about the thief.

To put it simply, the power of life and death isn't in the hands of some
external force; it's in your own hands. Are you ready to explore this idea
further? Instead of just taking my word for it, we're going to examine this
concept.

Let's look into the Bible to find evidence. According to 1 Corinthians 3:12–18, our actions and decisions are like building materials: gold, silver, and precious stones, or less valuable items like wood, hay, and straw. Our choices become obvious in the face of challenges, as if tested by fire.

Every person's work will be put to the test by fire to see its quality. If it burns up, you will lose your reward but still be saved, as though escaping through flames. However, if your work survives the fire, you will receive a reward. Remember, you are the temple of God, and His spirit lives within you. Therefore, if anyone damages God's temple, which means harming the work built on the foundation of Christ or misusing his or her body, the person invites God's displeasure. This implies that God's power is not aligned with evil, and in fact, life and death are influenced by our own words, not by evil forces. Thus, if evil tries to harm you, it does so by convincing you that you are not what God says you are. When you start behaving contrary to your true identity, you disrespect God's temple. You bring defilement upon the temple of God and at that point, it becomes legal for the temple to be destroyed, not because Satan has dominion, but because you walk in ignorance.

The power of your choices is greater than anything Satan can do. Remember, his intent is always to deceive, kill, steal, and destroy, and he doesn't play by the rules. Satan may try to lie to you. He has been defeated, but he'll still attempt to whisper lies to lead you astray. This can make you act in ways that are not true to yourself and corrupt what is holy. In earlier discussions, we talked about how wrongdoing, or iniquity, harms people. It's not because God wants to punish us, but because natural consequences to our actions are set in motion by God's principles. The warning was clear: 'If you eat from the forbidden tree, you will surely die'. It wasn't a threat from God but a natural outcome. Interestingly, scripture places the blame for humanity's downfall on Adam's decision, not on Satan. This shows that Adam's choice was more impactful than Satan's influence. In the same way, for Christians, the choices we make are more powerful than any of Satan's schemes.

Today, I want to infuse your spirit with a boost of divine energy. The true strength to make choices doesn't come from within us; it's fuelled by a force much greater. However, once you decide to act, nothing can hold you back. If you're reborn in Christ, remember that your only limit is your own determination, not the devil. You've given the devil too much credit. When his time comes to an end, you'll realize he wasn't as formidable as you thought. By focusing too much on him, you unwittingly give him power. He seems bigger because of the attention you give him, not because of his actual deeds. Many things blamed on him have nothing to do with him, but he benefits from being thought of as such a big deal. There are ministries that spend too much time talking about the devil, making him seem more important than he is.

Dive into the New Testament, and you'll discover it doesn't offer any basis for a believer to fear Satan. When Scripture mentions Satan, the message is clear: stay alert and sober. Keeping your eyes open means Satan has no power over you. Jesus illustrated this with the parable of the watchful homeowner, emphasizing that vigilance is key to prevention. Understanding the authority and power granted to us by Christ is all that's needed to keep watch effectively. Once this knowledge is firmly in place, Satan's influence dwindles.

Satan might try to scare us with minor disturbances, like the sound of leaves rustling at night, but these fears are often the result of our own unfounded beliefs. For instance, if you hear an owl at 2 a.m. singing a hymn, instead of recognizing God's creation, you might react in fear. This response gives Satan the leverage he needs, powered by your fear, to intimidate you further.

Don't magnify demons. Just gain spiritual knowledge.

My friend, do you find yourself overly worried about Satan, fearing he's out to get you? Someone once came to me, panicked, claiming Satan was after her, trying to end her life. I asked her, 'Why would Satan target you? What are you doing that's so threatening to him? Are you actively spreading God's word in a way that challenges Satan'? It would seem more logical for Satan to target me, someone actively sharing the gospel, rather than someone not involved in such work. I represent a bigger threat to him. Who would he choose if it came down to you or me? She laughed at this. It's not about boasting but understanding your place in Christ. The Bible reminds us to see ourselves accurately. There was a time when my nights were spent combating the devil. Thankfully, by God's grace, those days are behind me. Now, my prayers are centred on loving Jesus and Him alone.

When you spend time meditating on the precepts of God, Satan will not have a foothold. Satan should never be the subject of your prayers, but this comes as a product of growth. If you know what the Word of God says, and you also know what I know, then you will also be in a position to do what I do to live a life of peace in Christ.

Hebrews 2:15 explains that Jesus died to defeat the devil, who had the power of death, and to set free those who were scared of dying their whole lives. This means Jesus not only rescued you from being trapped but also told you that the devil used your fear of death against you. This shows that you don't need to wait for a future change to live without fear. Your real problem is not death itself, but the fear of it. Knowing you are saved should naturally free you from being afraid of death. This knowledge should empower you to face crises with courage, just like the apostles, who chose to stand firm rather than flee, driven by the strength of their mission even in tough times, did.

First Corinthians 3:17–18 teaches that anyone who corrupts what is meant to be sacred will face consequences, as we are considered holy temples. It warns against self-deception and the folly of worldly wisdom, suggesting that true wisdom comes from humility and a readiness to learn.

This passage highlights that wisdom valued by society can distract us from truly important spiritual truths. Being wealthy or intelligent isn't what makes someone significant in the spiritual realm. Instead, it's how one uses his or her resources or knowledge to support spiritual goals that counts.

For instance, Apostle Paul, despite being highly educated and a top student of Gamaliel, chose to use his knowledge to defend his faith and spread spiritual teachings. His life wasn't about boasting his previous status or wealth, but about promoting values that mattered on a deeper level. Through his teachings, he challenges us to reconsider our priorities and not be misled by material success or societal standards of wisdom. This encourages focusing on what genuinely enriches our spiritual lives rather than being distracted by worldly achievements.

Many of you worry not about having food, but about not having as much as your neighbours. I encourage you to take control of your life. True happiness comes from this control. When you believe that you are everything God says you are, and that is enough, you'll find contentment. You'll wear your only shirt with pride, iron it nicely, and walk confidently among important people. You'll say, 'I'm not in this shirt because I'm poor, but because it's suitable for now'. When the time comes, and you have twenty shirts, you won't feel more valuable than you do now. This is the beginning of true peace. The things that used to trouble you will no longer affect you, and you'll be forever changed. You'll realize that missing something someone else has doesn't make you lesser. That negative feeling I rebuke in the name of Jesus.

Friends, here's the truth according to God's divine plan: you are not truly ready for prosperity until prosperity can no longer change who you are at your core. That very thing making you feel less than enough? If you were to be blessed with wealth now, it might harm you instead. As it's said, anyone who harms his or her own integrity faces consequences. Sometimes, you might not receive certain blessings because you need to be prepared for them first. It's not about denial; it's about being built up so that prosperity doesn't lead you astray. Pride is met with resistance, not from the forces against us but from the God Himself. Remember, this resistance isn't meant to put you down. If you are truly aligned with God, being humbled is necessary to be of true service.

Why is God speaking in this way? Because He is focused on flourishing His church. The time for action is now. God is moving swiftly and efficiently in His goodness. After reading this book, many of your previous fears will no longer bother you. This is because God needs to complete His work in you quickly to provide you with your inheritance.

In the kingdom of God, what is seen as wise often looks foolish to the world. Remember, the world's wisdom is foolishness to God. This is because, as stated in scripture, God outsmarts the so-called wise in their cunning. Have you ever thought about how our fears are often tied to worldly wisdom? Every fear that troubles you is rooted in the world's way of thinking. Once you accept this as true wisdom, you will put all your effort into achieving it. For instance, have you felt disrespected because you lack money or power? I have been there, thinking if only I had more, I'd be treated better, and my feelings of inadequacy would disappear. However, when I realized that gaining respect through what I could offer did not actually fix my deeper feelings of inadequacy, it was a turning point. I found that among those who valued what I had, it didn't really matter after all. The insecurities I hoped to escape quickly returned.

I am complete in Christ!

Learn to value what truly matters. Don't let the fear of tomorrow control you. This is what true freedom means. Such freedom is found in meekness and a lowly heart. If you go on a vacation not planned by God and spend all your money, you'll find yourself in trouble, filled with worry. You need to liberate yourself from this. Some people save money, fearing future illnesses and believing security comes from how much they have saved. I'm not saying you shouldn't have medical insurance; that would be unwise. However, understand that living in fear is influenced by harmful beliefs. Jesus taught us not to accumulate earthly wealth, which can be stolen or destroyed. Instead, focus on gathering your riches in heaven, where they are safe from harm.

You might wonder how you can store up treasures in heaven. Jesus said to us that our treasure follows where our heart values most. This implies that even if I have KES twenty billion, I wouldn't worry about being cheated out of it. That's because my real treasure isn't in the bank; it's in Christ.

Can I share something that the church has preached for so long that may shake you to your core? Many of you have often heard that tithing is the way to find peace and overflow. However, the underlying reason for your tithing seems to be based more on fear than on faith and love. Notice how when you don't tithe, your pay check seems to run out by mid-month. However, if you do tithe, your money stretches further, often until the next pay check arrives. You might be thinking of Malachi 3 now. Yet, the real question is if God is our Father, shouldn't our actions honour Him? Tithing should be about honouring God, not just seeking protection. When the Bible talks about money disappearing as though there are holes in our pockets, it's not saying tithing patches those holes. Instead, it suggests that turning away from God leads to loss. Missing out on tithing is not about facing constant punishment; it's about where our hearts are in relation to God. It's okay if this truth is hard to accept. After all, in these challenging times, only the truth will stand firm.

If you don't understand these concepts, even your actions intended to honour God can be rooted in fear. Fear creates an opportunity for negativity to take hold. Once fear enters, it opens a door, transferring power that should belong to you, the believer, away from you. This allows negative forces to influence you, not because they are strong, but because your life is governed by fear. Fear is the doorway to this shift in power.

First Corinthians 3:20 (NIV) highlights a meaningful insight.

> The Lord knows the thoughts of the wise and finds them lacking substance. Therefore, no one should boast about following particular human leaders. Everything belongs to you—Paul, Apollos, Cephas, the world, life, death, the present, or the future. All of it is yours, and you belong to Christ, who belongs to God.

You can't take pride in being a disciple of someone like Dr. Myles Monroe. The only true source of pride is knowing the same God that Dr. Myles Munroe knew. This means your faith and trust shouldn't rely solely on human guidance. While it's a good starting point, your faith should evolve beyond human mentors to discover God for yourself. God is more powerful than any mentor or leader. Rather than leaning entirely on others' insights, dedicate your time to exploring and understanding God, who empowered those you look up to and made them influential.

Remember, in a believer's life, Satan does not hold the power of death. The only way Satan can have any control over death concerning a believer is through the fear of death. If a believer fears death, it indicates he or she does not fully understand what Christ has freed him or her from.

It's crucial to recognize the anger you might feel knowing how much fear and trouble have been caused in your life. You should not have to deal with fear at all.

CHAPTER 12

THE FALLACY OF THE FOE

Unmasking Deceit

I want us to go back and address the four aspects of fear that we discussed in chapter 7, and I'll explain how each one has been overcome by Christ.

Friends, this is your moment. The door to your freedom and perfect liberty in Christ is now fully open. Walk in and take all that's been given to you in Christ Jesus!

In the four engagements of God with Adam, it was evident that Adam did not experience any kind of fear. Let us go back there and allow the Holy Spirit to set us free.

1. OVERCOMING THE FEAR OF INSUFFICIENCY

God created Adam from the dust and breathed life into him, making him alive. Afterward, God prepared a special place called Eden and planted a beautiful garden there. It's important to note that God provided everything before placing Adam there. This shows us that God ensures our needs are met first.

I hope that you are aware that Adam was created before the garden was ready. However, by the time Adam arrived in the garden, it was fully prepared with everything he might need. He could enjoy all the fruits and everything in the garden except for one rule: not to eat from the Tree of Knowledge of Good and Evil. Before Eve joined him, Adam didn't question this rule or wonder about the forbidden tree.

This story highlights how God takes care of our needs, preparing our provision even before we realize we need it.

Breaking a commandment doesn't mean the commandment is wrong, as explained in Romans 7. It suggests there's something off within us. Commandments existed even before humans first sinned. For example, God told Adam not to eat from a certain tree, and Adam didn't question it. God explained that eating from the tree would lead to death, yet this wasn't about instilling fear of death. It shows that fear of punishment, like the fear of hell, won't be what ultimately saves people. Being scared of hell doesn't prevent anyone from ending up there.

When God created Adam and noticed he was alone, it raised an interesting question. Did God already know that Adam would need a companion? Yes, He did. Despite this, Adam was still considered perfect. When it came time to create a companion for Adam, God didn't look elsewhere; He created woman from man. This shows that just because Adam needed something didn't mean he was flawed.

If Adam had complained to God about being alone, it could seem like he was critiquing God's creation. However, consider this scenario: if I review work from my assistant and say it's not good enough, it's not necessarily a criticism of her effort. Instead, I'm recognizing her potential to achieve more because I know her capabilities. Even if her work was praised by others, only she and I would know if she could have done better.

This means that when God saw what He had created, He saw it as an opportunity for improvement, not as a criticism. Similarly, when someone tells you that you've made a mistake, you shouldn't feel attacked but see it as a chance to do better. Remember, feeling criticized and attacked in the past likely came from fear, from Satan, and not from a place of constructive feedback.

Let me share a short narrative that will explain this. Juma stood rigid among the swaying bodies of the faithful. In this small church, the air was thick with hymns and the scent of polished wooden pews. As the congregation rose for offerings, a river of worshippers streamed down the aisle, each person lost in his or her devotion, giving in to the joy of song and dance.

There stood Juma, his facade as unblemished as the Sunday suit that gripped his broad shoulders, the rapture of praise barely brushing against him. He believed that men of stature, men with businesses and respect—the big men—held themselves with a gravity that made such displays frivolous. Dancing and singing before the crowd seemed, to him, to chip away at the hard-earned dignity he displayed.

People clapped and danced their way to give their offerings—all except Juma, who walked with a stoic stride, lips sealed, silently insisting that his reverence needn't be performed. Then came a voice. 'Brother Juma', called out the pastor, and a hush fell upon the congregation. Eyes flicked back and forth between the poised man and their leader. 'Tell me, Brother Juma, why do we not see your feet dance? Why does your voice not join the chorus?' Juma, usually so composed, felt a bead of sweat travel from his temple to his stiff collar. There was nowhere to hide as scores of eyes pinned him in place. The pastor's smile never faded, yet his eyes locked onto Juma with the gentle force of ageless wisdom. 'Yes, we all know of your successes, Brother Juma', he said, the air around him alight with tender amusement. 'We, too, know how to behave like big men, but remember, it is not to each other that we dance or sing. It is for the Lord'.

How do you think Juma felt?

Juma did not only feel shame; he felt angry, spited, and unwanted. Maybe it would have been his last day to go church. What Juma did not understand, though, was that everything that sounded like criticism was an open door to him, reminding him that God created him to be greater and better than this. You will now find out that fear does not only take a hold on us but it also becomes the lens by which we see, the ear from which we hear, and the mind from which we interpret actions.

Many of you are afraid of being corrected, and this fear either keeps you from serving to avoid correction or makes you tense. This means you can't freely express yourself, even in places where freedom should reign supreme.

For some, fear has crept in because of the negative opinions and words others have directed at you. This has made you timid and hesitant, lowering your confidence and belief in your abilities. Remember, any force that diminishes your effectiveness is not from a good place; it's rooted in fear. Words spoken against you, almost like a spell, have started to shake your faith in what you believed. I stand against these negative voices. Every harsh word aimed at you, I condemn in the name of Jesus. Any voice telling you that you can't, that you are not enough, or that you are disqualified because of who you are, I oppose those lies in the mighty name of Jesus, with the powerful backing of His blood.

Some of you may feel trapped in marriages that seem to limit you, but my intention is not to encourage rebellion. Instead, I want to inspire you to rise above those constraints. To those who feel belittled or held back by their spouses, I declare in the powerful name of Jesus that every negative word and boundary set against you is broken. I proclaim that you are infused with the courage and boldness of Jesus, empowering you to move beyond fear, right now, in Jesus's name. Remember, the Bible tells us not to lose our confidence because it comes with great reward. Whenever you have felt your confidence slip away, I, through God's intervention, reclaim it for you. I decree, in the name of Jesus, you will lift your head high.

The Lord embodies the Spirit. Thus, if any other spirit seeks your attention, you have to weigh its authority against the Lord's, under whose guidance you stand. This explains why, when someone preaches in Jesus's name and authorities or the government object, saying he or she can't use Jesus's name there, you shouldn't fear. You simply question who made this rule. If they say it's the government or parliament, your reply should be that your reverence for Jesus outweighs any fear of governmental powers. If threats come your way, turn to prayer, asking the Lord for boldness to continue spreading His word, despite opposition. The early believers never prayed to avoid persecution; instead, they prayed for the courage to perform miracles and preach boldly in Jesus's name. They asked the Lord to perform miracles by their hands as a sign of who has sent them. They only feared the Lord—no one else. Where the Lord's Spirit is, there is freedom, liberating us from any other fears by knowing we are protected by the Lord.

This is why being meek and lowly of heart sets you free. If God tells me to start a church in Mukuru kwa Njenga despite local powers saying it is not possible, my response would be simple. I'll tell God, 'Look, they're trying to scare us'. I wouldn't worry about their threats. Instead, I would ask God to show even greater miracles through me. This way, those trying to intimidate us will realize that there is only one true Lord I follow.

Second Timothy 1:6–7 reminds us to rekindle the gifts God has placed within us through faith. It tells us God didn't give us spirits of fear, but rather ones of power, love, and sound mind. Fear holds you back, making you believe you are not enough and what you have is not valuable. If you fail to remember and nurture God's gift within you, it remains unused. Fear can make you feel inadequate, but recalling God's gifts can help you overcome this.

Many readers of this book are talented and fortunate. However, when you visit places, you might feel that others perform better at the tasks you do. By giving in to this intimidation, fear starts to overshadow your abilities, leading you to believe others are superior. Remember, God didn't ask you to outperform or underperform. He simply wants you to just do it! God teaches us three key lessons to overcome fear.

a. **Power:** In many situations where fear tries to overpower you, what you need is the display of God's power. Consider how the disciples responded to threats by praying, 'Lord, please show your power and perform miracles through your Holy Son Jesus'. This shows us that the response to being scared or intimidated is to demonstrate power. The solution to fear is indeed power.

b. **Love:** In the space of love, you believe all things, hope all things, and strive for everything God guides you toward. If you love Him, you will obey His commands. Often, you'll find yourself doing so even when your love falters.

c. **A sound mind:** This means having the freedom and ability to arrive at the right decisions and judgements about all matters. It liberates you from fear.

I decree and declare, in the name of the Lord Jesus, every gift that has laid dormant because of intimidation and fear, I command the stirring of your waters now. I decree in the name of the Lord Jesus that by working of the hand of the Lord, you will rise from the place of obscurity and enter into the place of the manifestation of the fullness of God.

Thank you, Father.

Some of you might be worried about what tomorrow brings because you're not fully trusting in the One who promises a bright path for the righteous. I believe that my ministry will continue to grow stronger each day. I'm not concerned about waking up one day to find no one listening to my podcast or reading my book. My purpose isn't rooted in popularity; it's in living to please the Lord. If no one reads my book today, there are still countless ways to serve Jesus. Therefore, Satan can't intimidate me by saying no one is following or listening. How will I succeed? My confidence doesn't come from being able to write a book. Everything I have accomplished is thanks to the Lord and His guidance through others. I am confident because God has lifted me up and will continue to support me. God doesn't make futile investments. After witnessing what God has done in my life, I cannot be fearful of what the future holds. I focus on the present, serving God's purpose each day, rather than worrying about an uncertain tomorrow.

I save and prepare for when God's need will show up, trusting in God's plan for future needs, knowing I have no reserves for unexpected troubles. Doubts and fears are overcome by faith. Sometimes I wonder what's the worst that could happen if I run out of money tomorrow? The ultimate fear might be death, but for me, that means joining heaven, as to live is Christ and to die is gain, bringing me home to my Maker. However, I believe my time has not come yet, for I have a mission to fulfil, dedicated to bringing glory to my King.

It's important to understand these ideas. Honestly, whenever I find myself worried about death due to negative thoughts, it's the well-being of the living that concerns me most. Wanting to leave this world without considering the impact and leaving behind pain feels selfish, especially when I've been blessed with so much. Remember, the idea of evil being everywhere is not true. Satan is defeated! You have already won over such negativity. It only has power if you allow it into your heart.

2. OVERCOMING THE FEAR OF NEED

The gripping fear of need often hinders the average believer from placing his or her trust in God. True reliance on God means facing our challenges without trembling in fear. It's about crying out with confidence, 'Hear my cry, O Lord; listen to my prayer'. We might be tempted to plead out of desperation, 'Lord, save me'! Yet, a deeper spiritual understanding guides each of us to instead declare, 'When my heart is overwhelmed, lead me to the rock that is higher than me'.

Why this approach? Because the pressures of life, especially when you feel oppressed and pushed to a corner, can distort your perception, making you lose sight of the fact that God's view is not the same as yours. From His perspective, your trials are not obstacles but opportunities shaping your destiny. God has always been your refuge, a formidable bastion against life's upheavals.

David understood this when he proclaimed God as his shelter and strong tower, a place where he found safety amidst chaos. Similarly, our lives include pressure not to crush us but to reveal the significant breakthroughs that lie ahead. Every past instance when you've taken shelter in God's name becomes a testament to His unwavering protection.

Therefore, as believers, we should not stand amid our tribulations, helplessly crying out for rescue from death. Our focus ought to be on discerning our circumstances through God's eyes, not merely on escaping them. This perspective shift offers the assurance and boldness needed to endure and ultimately witness the unfolding of His divine plan.

Your faith makes you a master over storms.

Reflect on this scenario. If the disciples had refrained from waking Jesus during the tempest, what could have occurred? With Jesus aboard, the storm certainly would not have bested them; instead, it would have carried them safely to their intended destination. It's important to recognize that Jesus performed miracles not for His own sake, but to aid others. This mirrors the scriptural promise in Psalms 23:5 (NIV), which states, 'You prepare a table before me in the presence of my enemies'. This signifies God's sustenance and safeguarding amidst adversity. In the same vein, you as a believer are called to do more than merely halt storms; you are to command authority over them. Drawing strength from the declaration, 'Rule in the midst of your enemies' (Psalm 110:1–3), you are reminded that, through steadfast faith, you have the power to dominate your trials.

When you arrive at perfect peace, you revel in the knowledge that the storms cannot reach your soul. It is crucial to acknowledge that you belong to an Almighty God, one who protects you with His rod and staff. Whose service commands your loyalty? In God's service, self-ownership must yield. I stand as a bond servant, distinct from any employee. My commitment is enduring. An employee concludes work at day's end, while a bond servant's life is woven into the very fabric of his or her master's domain. For me, there is no final hour to my charge; at a summons, even at 2:00 a.m., I am present. Thus, my safeguard is intertwined with my master's protection. Should my master be secure, so too shall I be free from harm.

If you could truly grasp the extent of power at your disposal through your actions, your words, and your beliefs, you would never concede any advantage to Satan.

3. OVERCOMING THE FEAR OF THE UNKNOWN

Adam was presented with creatures he had never encountered before, yet he named them instinctively, as if tapping into a divine understanding. This mirrors the sentiment shared in the preceding chapter, where I emphasized the purpose of the Holy Spirit to impart wisdom on the unknown and to rekindle memories of what has been learned and perhaps forgotten. It underscores the profound truth that a believer is perpetually equipped with knowledge.

My friends, the emotional response elicited by the unknown is greatly influenced by the individual concealing your vision. Allow me to clarify. Imagine being confronted by an abductor wielding a firearm, dictating your compliance, and obscuring your sight. In such a scenario, each tentative step you take is shrouded in escalating fear. The captor is well aware that fear intensifies when you're deprived of sight. Contrastingly, envision your significant other suggesting a surprise and asking if he or she can cover your eyes. With each step guided by trust, anticipation replaces apprehension, and excitement burgeons as you eagerly anticipate the reveal. Thus, the emotion stirred by the unknown pivots on the identity of the one who obscures your view, inspiring either a crescendo of fear or the thrill of anticipation. It's the intention behind the concealed view that dictates our emotional states.

Facing the unknown need not be a source of fear for you, the believer. Instead, embrace the unfamiliar, for within it often lies a delightful surprise orchestrated by God Himself. Consider that in matters of the heart and love, God delights in the role of the one planning the surprise, revelling in His nature as a God brimming with wonder. Do not cower before the unknown; take courage instead. It is said, 'Because He lives, I can face tomorrow'. Proclaim with confidence that although the future may be unknown, your trust resides in the One who tenderly holds your days to come. In that trust, find your peace; it is more than sufficient.

4. OVERCOMING THE FEAR OF INADEQUACY AND RESTLESSNESS

The world might echo the sentiment that you are not enough. Each glance levelled your way can come across as judgemental, planting the seed of doubt within you. This nagging insecurity stifles the potential that God envisions for you, which we have extensively discussed concerning other fears. It's imperative to break free from the futile exercise of comparing your achievements to those of others.

Consider this. No parent holds the same expectations for two children of different ages. It would be unreasonable for me to expect my three-year-old to lug a bucket of water, just as it would be preposterous for him to weep in frustration because his ten-year-old sibling can. There's an age for bearing burdens and an age for having them borne for you. Savour the moments when others shoulder the load. Soon enough, you'll be the one doing the carrying.

Frequently, feelings of inadequacy arise from our tendency to compare ourselves to others. Our sense of self-worth remains unchallenged until we encounter someone who exceeds our abilities—by standards we've set for ourselves. It's crucial to detach our self-perception from others' judgements. Often, what we believe to be the opinions of others is actually a reflection of our own insecurities and not their actual thoughts. Striving for autonomy from external validation allows us to experience true freedom. Arrive at liberty from the opinion of others.

Many struggle with restless nights, burdened by worries and fears. Psalm 127:2 (NIV) suggests that toiling from dawn until dusk, consumed by anxieties (what the text calls 'the bread of sorrows') is futile because true rest is a gift from God to His beloved.

Understand that sleep here symbolizes more than just time spent in slumber; it's about the peace within your soul. A mere three hours of restful sleep can be more rejuvenating than ten hours of fitful restlessness. Achieving this peace is addressed in 2 Timothy 6. Internalize the wisdom that life's essence isn't measured by material wealth. According to scripture, true fulfilment is found in godliness accompanied by contentment.

Being godly does not mean lacking purpose, ambition, or vision. Rather, it involves a sense of thankfulness for the present and a confident assurance that tomorrow holds greater prospects secured by God's hands.

Hebrews 13:5 (NIV) urges us to lead lives free from the love of money, encouraging us to find contentment in our present circumstances with the assurance that God has promised, 'Never will I leave you; never will I forsake you'. This echoes Psalm 46:1 (NIV), which proclaims that God is our refuge and strength, an ever-present help during difficult times. Understand that God isn't merely a bystander; He actively provides support. It's crucial to recognize and trust in God's omnipresent love and care.

Your soul must cultivate confidence in the unwavering presence of God and in His deep love for you, so profound that He would not idly observe you endure suffering without intervening. I urge you to listen with the depth of your spirit. Many Christians harbour doubts about God. The uncertainty regarding His will in your life undermines your ability to trust Him completely. We must learn to wholly commit ourselves to God's hands, trusting in His divine purpose.

Do you recall the classic trust fall exercise? It's when you ask a trusted individual to stand behind you, and then you fall back with full confidence, not needing to look back to verify the person's position. The understanding is that when you lean back, that person will catch you, preventing any injury. However, if the person fails to catch you, it's a sign that he or she is not trustworthy.

Isn't it intriguing how life has led us to trust inert objects, such as chairs or even volatile things like the stock market, more than beings capable of making conscious choices?

In contemplation, if I were to undertake the trust fall again, I might opt for purchasing a strong rope and rigging a net where I can safely fall, certain of its support. This trust stems from the net's inability to make a decision, unlike a person who can choose whether to catch you or not.

This analogy extends to our faith, suggesting that any hesitance in trusting God is rooted in our uncertainties about His intentions. It implies that believers struggle with fully relying on God's will because of a lack of confidence in His inherent goodness and assurance that He prioritizes our well-being. Consequently, they can't fully surrender, casting all doubts aside and trusting God implicitly in every aspect of their lives.

Can I tell you that your reluctance to fully extend yourself and surrender to God signals that your mind insists on carving paths for every situation in your life, robbing you of restful sleep? Pause and reflect!

Trusting in God's will is foundational to overcoming doubt in His purpose for you. Take time to deeply study God's will, for by understanding it, you'll find assurance in His intentions. Jeremiah 29:11 (NIV) assures us that He has plans for us, plans for prosperity and not harm, plans to give us hope and a future. When you place your trust in God's will, you free yourself from the weight of trying to manage every detail of your existence. True peace comes only when you recognize that God's wisdom, which may seem foolish to the world, is far superior to any human knowledge.

We are on a path to achieving perfect peace. Despite our proclamations, the underlying principles still exert their influence. Even if I were to make declarations and lay hands on you until your head became as smooth as a cue ball, it doesn't alter the fact that you would continue to live in fear if you do not grasp what is referred to as 'the will of God'. Understanding this concept means recognizing that you may walk through darkness yet still be in perfect peace, for you know who guides your steps.

No number of declarations I make can prevent difficulties from coming your way. In fact, some of the adversities that beset you might have been crafted by God and handed over to Satan for delivery. This is because the divine purposes ordained to unfold on Earth often necessitate traversing through such trials. God is not taken aback by the challenges you face. What concerns Him is when your heart is fretful in the midst of them. Such anxiety betrays a loss of awareness of the constant presence of God alongside you.

The root of distrust in God often lurks behind the concept of 'the will of God'. The paradox lies in the fact that people struggle to trust God precisely because He has a will of His own. However, when you truly know God, His will becomes the very foundation of your trust in Him.

CHAPTER 13

SOVEREIGNTY OF THE WILL

The Strength to Choose

At the start of the book, it was shared by the Lord that several factors contribute to becoming enslaved, one key factor being when sin is iniquity. As we saw, iniquity is not just about personal wrongdoings. Every action against the law or failure to follow God's laws impacts the world. Often, those who were not even involved in the wrongdoing can suffer from its consequences. According to 1 Corinthians 15 (NIV), just as disobedience by one person (referring to Adam) introduced sin and death into the world, obedience by another (referring to Jesus) offers everyone the chance to be righteous.

Death was not part of God's original design; it resulted from human choice. When Adam and Eve ate from the tree they were warned against (the tree offering knowledge of what's good and evil), they set in motion their own mortality. This action led to every form of death, whether it be the end of life or the separation between people and God. Essentially, cessation of life was a direct consequence of separation from God. Therefore, no person was meant to experience death. Only the decision to eat from that specific tree caused mortality to become a reality for humankind.

One might ask why God placed the Tree of Knowledge of Good and Evil in the garden. To simplify the explanation, consider how some medications are labelled as not suitable for children under twelve years of age. This is because a child under this age may not be physically ready to safely handle the medication's effects. The child's body still needs to mature enough to process the ingredients. Similarly, something intended to be beneficial can be harmful if not used at the right time or in the right way. Although Adam was created perfectly, he still had to grow into a certain level of maturity and understanding. This principle is mirrored in how Jesus was brought into the world through a virgin birth, bypassing the inherited nature of sin and representing the completion of God's perfect creation in human form.

Friends, I want you to understand something important. Sinning isn't just about having a sinful nature. Even without it, people can still choose to sin because of the free will that God has given us. The Bible tells us that once we commit ourselves to Christ, we're reborn not from human desire but as children of God. This means that our original sinful nature doesn't control us anymore. It's as if it no longer exists from the moment we decide to follow Christ. However, the ability to choose (our free will) doesn't go away. This freedom to make choices, known as free will, is key in our relationships with God. It's God's way of showing His love, by allowing us to decide whether to follow Him. Remember, every choice we make has its consequences. It's based on what we know, just like how Eve was influenced because she was told eating the fruit would bring pleasure.

Keep in mind, Adam was not inherently sinful, yet he still committed sin. It's crucial to grasp this concept.

Culture often exerts a force more potent than nature itself. For example, humans are naturally inclined to walk upright, but through cultural influence, it's possible to train individuals to adopt behaviours far removed from their natural tendencies. The story of Tarzan, a boy raised by animals and adopting their behaviours, illustrates this well. For Tarzan, moving on all fours and communicating like his animal family felt normal. In contrast, for those raised in human societies, such actions seem odd because they deviate from the behaviours we've been taught to recognize as human. This concept extends to current cultural debates, such as the acceptance of LGBTQI identities, where what is unnatural and displeasureable has become recognized as pleasurable and valued. We are now at a point where if you are not accepting of the LGBTQI community, you are viewed with disdain, disgust, and anger.

Some things can be hard to deal with and aren't even appealing. I want to address the men out there. Are you aware of the inherent beauty in women, how they've been delicately and meticulously created? This appreciation should extend to all women, not just your spouse. However, considering the vast array of beautiful women around, it's bewildering when someone still looks elsewhere, especially toward another man. This is unthinkable! No matter what, a woman, regardless of her appearance, is more appealing than a man who, due to overindulgence, changes his physique. This notion is simply wrong. The idea that LGBTQI is even a topic for discussion is absurd and indicates a deep-seated brokenness in humanity.

Culture often has a stronger influence than our natural instincts. This explains why merely relying on the inner change from being 'born again' is not sufficient for living as Christ did. Romans 12:1 advises us to dedicate our bodies to God, living in purity and holiness. It warns against conforming to worldly behaviours, emphasizing the importance of transforming our minds rather than our inherent natures. The Message Bible puts it succinctly by advising us not to become so well adjusted to our culture that we fit into it without even thinking. Instead, fix your attention on God. You'll be changed from the inside out. Readily recognize what God wants from you, and quickly respond to it. Unlike the culture around you, always dragging you down to its level of immaturity, God brings the best out of you, and develops well-formed maturity in you. Essentially, what captures our attention has a greater impact than our basic makeup.

Heavenly matters should enrich you, but this doesn't happen simply by divine intervention. Instead, when you engage in worship, you start finding more joy in spiritual activities than ordinary ones. This joy is what you're seeking when you reach out with open hands in worship. However, it's important to continue living by these higher principles. If you just go back to your everyday habits after prayer and worship, chances are you will forget the experience. This suggests that your mind plays a bigger role in shaping who you are than your spirit does. Your true essence lies within your spirit, but it will not manifest until your mind understands what's taking place on a spiritual level. If your mind focuses more on physical experiences than on spiritual ones, no amount of positive talk will change your negative life's direction away from God's intentions for you.

We now realize that our culture has a greater influence on us than our innate qualities. Adam, created directly by God without human parents, was a child of God released into the world. This shows that when it comes to saving you, God isn't concerned with your biological lineage. What really matters is whose authority of thought you choose to follow. When people seek freedom, they often abandon all structure, equating freedom with chaos. They do this to avoid feeling controlled. This concept goes beyond simply being spiritually reborn.

Where did Satan deceive Eve? He did not deny God's wisdom; instead, he suggested to Eve that she was still being controlled by God, and that was the trap. Eve desired to gain her freedom and think for herself, believing this would liberate her. However, it is important to realize that true freedom comes with order. More often than not, when you believe you are seeking freedom, you are actually stepping into a form of bondage. This happens when you try to break away from thoughts or rules that you feel limit you. Romans 7 discusses the struggle between what you want to do and what you are told is wrong. The moment you are told not to do something, a rebellious spirit can awaken within you because you feel controlled. You think that by exploring on your own terms, you can make better decisions. Yet, oftentimes, you find that what you had before was better than what you sought.

At that point, you have become trapped, and this new master is far different from the first one. While the first Master allows you the freedom to choose, the second one restricts you with bonds, making you repeat actions you would rather avoid. This is in line with what the scripture in James says about looking deep into the perfect law of liberty. What truly liberates you is a law that's been refined to perfection. Thus, liberty is not simply about having choices. It is about adopting a law that's been thoroughly tested and proven to consistently yield the best possible results for your life. God didn't create us to wander aimlessly on Earth. As Ecclesiastes explains, our lifetimes are too brief for endless exploration. We are given this time to develop trust in God, to see God's outcomes, and to trust them enough to willingly follow God's perfect law. This is crucial because there is no condemnation for those in Christ Jesus who live by the spirit, not by worldly desires. The law of the spirit of life in Christ Jesus, the perfect law, frees us from the grip of sin and death. Remember, sin and death operate under their own law.

Allow me to put this in unforgettable terms: no one is truly independent or free. Everyone answers to some authority. Whoever advised you to break away from God's law was merely positioning himself or herself to take control over you and become your master.

The universe operates under certain rules. Once you stray from the ultimate rule of freedom, which is God's law, you find yourself trapped in a cycle of control and dependency. In this situation, addiction plays a role as the devil plants seeds of doubt in your mind. He suggests that your actions are merely fulfilling the role of a slave to God. He then claims that God's love for you is not as genuine as His love for Himself, suggesting that by eating the forbidden fruit, you would attain god-like status. This implies that God might be withholding this power to maintain dominance over you. The devil deceives you into thinking he is offering liberation, giving you the power of choice. However, once you step outside God's protection, you quickly realize you are under the influence of a different ruler. The devil ensures you lose the way back to God, making the sinful acts seem appealing and suggesting a greater satisfaction lies ahead. From the beginning, though, there is an underlying dissatisfaction, but the devil convinces you there is more to be discovered, leading to a point of no return, possibly into addiction.

This illustrates why turning back, or repentance, is a step of faith.

One of the key reasons why God forgives all our mistakes as soon as we show genuine remorse is because acknowledging our need to find our way back from darkness requires remarkable spiritual strength. This acknowledgement is crucial because the greatest deception by evil forces is convincing us that we are beyond redemption. This concept is similar to the lesson from the parable of the prodigal son, which might not make sense without this understanding. Growing up, I often thought the father's acceptance of the younger son was unjust toward the elder son, who seemed to have a right to be upset. However, the father honoured the bravery it took for his younger son to decide to come back home from a place filled with negative influences, like substance abuse and moral corruption. When the son returned, the father did not demand proof of change to restore his position in the family. The real test had already been passed the moment the son realized his mistakes and decided to return. By then, the father was ready to fully welcome him back, confident that his son had learned his lesson and valued what truly matters over fleeting temptations. This teaches us that real freedom is not about living without rules, but rather by choosing wisely the principles by which we want to live our lives. Every choice we make is governed by some form of law.

Every person is governed by a law. Choose wisely!

Be cautious of the enemy, the thief, who tries to convince you that you have not experienced the world fully. He will suggest that your obedience to God is only because you feel limited. Despite a deep desire to flee, you find yourself staying put but you would rather not be there. You want to run from God. In such moments, the God who promises to never leave you presents you with a choice between life and death. He advises you to choose life so that you may truly live. Only by making your own choices, rather than being forced into staying with God, that you find peace in your soul. The essence of genuine worship with Jesus is where you are free to choose, unlike with Satan who always tries to control you. This freedom of choice, which even Satan cannot override, is one of God's most significant blessings.

If the devil had his way, he would try to trap you with chains. Here's the thing: no chain from hell is stronger than the choices you make. There's no form of darkness or control the devil creates that can overpower your ability to choose. It is not about the power of the blood of Jesus, but about your decision. Yes, the blood of Jesus has power but it cannot override your personal will. If you decide to say it is over, then it is indeed over! It is not because of your strength, but because you know who to turn to for protection. He will not judge you for your past or your mistakes. Remember, no one can defeat the devil on his or her own, but no chain from hell can restrain a person who makes a single, simple decision. That is how significant your choices are, my friends.

Choose today, my dear friends, whom you will serve.

CHAPTER 14

REFLECTIONS AT JOURNEY'S END

A Conclusive Meditation

As we come to the final chapter of this book, I would like us to share in some finishing thoughts.

Matthew 11 (NIV) offers a profound message about the nature of rest in the context of faith. It suggests that rest doesn't simply come from ceasing our labours but by aligning ourselves with a greater purpose: God's purpose for our lives. When Jesus invites us to 'come unto me, all ye that labour and are heavy laden', He's offering reprieve not just from our immediate burdens but from the enduring weight we carry.

Often, we seek relief from our troubles, and while we may find temporary solace, without a deeper transformation, we remain vulnerable to life's relentless challenges. For many, this cycle is familiar: seeking healing and finding it, only to be met with new afflictions later on. This happens because Satan continuously seeks us out.

God encourages us to 'take my yoke upon you' (Matthew 11:28 NIV), which is an invitation to partnership rather than mere alleviation. The imagery of a yoke, typically shared by two oxen, implies that we are not meant to bear life's burdens alone. Joining with Jesus means that our struggles are shared, and no burden that falls upon us does so without also resting upon Him. This concept of a shared yoke teaches us about true rest, an intermingling of our efforts with the divine strength offered by Jesus. That means that nothing will rest upon you that will not have legality to rest upon Jesus.

When we talk about joining forces with Christ, it involves adopting His humility and gentle heart. When you do so, you'll discover that the load we associate with discipleship (His yoke) is seemingly light. However, the truth is, the yoke itself is not inherently easy, nor the burden naturally light. It's an uneven partnership where Jesus assumes the full weight of the yoke you were meant to carry. You are simply His companion as He shoulders the load.

This explains why so many tire out in their service to God; they approach it as if managing their own enterprise. To illuminate this point, consider a personal business, like Njeri Muchunu Global Limited. If it's mine, I'll guard it zealously because its failure means my loss. In essence, I serve there knowing that Christ accompanies me; otherwise, I would not risk proceeding.

My prayer then becomes, 'Lord, if Your presence isn't with me, I don't want to move forward. I need You close by as I head out, guiding me with Your love and grace. May Your presence energize my team and me every day, leading the way. To You, our God, we pray, show us Your glory, and may Your Presence travel with us'.

We feel overburdened because we mistakenly shoulder God's tasks as our personal ventures. Anyone who has tried to accomplish God's work through human effort alone understands its weight. However, the invitation we received wasn't to work; it was to yoke with Him. In our yoking, it's not the labour that's at the forefront, but rather the connection with our fellow bearers—the yoke mates. With Christ as my yoke mate, I am assured that He sustains most of the burden. He merely asks for my presence as a physical testament to His actions.

This is the essence of meekness. For instance, when you're on stage speaking, imagine Christ softly interrupting, whispering in your ear, 'Tell them I am forever breaking the power of fear'. Then, your role is simply to relay His message to the listeners: 'Christ is forever breaking the power of fear'.

The practice of walking with Jesus is one of trust and rest, knowing He is the one leading and carrying the day's difficulties. Our part is humble partnership, echoing His words, advancing in His strength, and recognizing it is His work we're privileged to partake in and never ours to bear alone.

In the above scenario, the question arises: who is the speaker? This inquiry dissipates when we understand that the challenge isn't to continuously conjure our next words or to actively seek revelation. Instead, our only necessary action is to remain steadfast in Him. By dwelling in His presence, the guidance we seek naturally becomes the driving force of our actions. Thus, His words are not merely spoken; they are propelled with purpose. The focal point of the narrative shifts to Him, rather than to ourselves. It's at this juncture that ministry unfolds with ease, proportional to the depth of our unity with Him. My friends, the gateway to rest for your souls lies in harnessing meekness and lowliness of heart.

Lowliness of heart leads to the recognition that success is not solely a product of one's own endeavours or exertion. On the other hand, meekness teaches us to patiently rely on the One who ultimately directs our efforts.

Many among us Christians struggle to find rest for our souls, often due to a tendency to rely more on our own intellect than on faith and trust in God. I implore you to consider this truth. Recall the moment Adam consumed the fruit from the Tree of the Knowledge of Good and Evil. In that instant, fear and the compulsion to solve his problems took root, robbing him of rest for his soul. Take this to heart: do not burden yourself with the obligation to find answers to questions that God has not posed to you. Resist the pressure, and instead, rest in the assurance of His guidance and timing.

Humanity never faced true adversity until encountering the fears of death, the fear of need, the fear of the unknown—all fears stemming from the consumption of the forbidden fruit from the Tree of Knowledge of Good and Evil. Prior to this event, there was no imperative for self-reliance or introspection. However, Christ has liberated us from the burdens pronounced by scriptural laws. Romans chapter 5 clarifies that the 'curse of the Law' does not refer to the Mosaic law. Yet, death held dominion over those who had not replicated Adam's sin—a sign that from birth we inherit the legacy of our ancestors' sins.

From the outset of life, individuals grapple with an inherited restlessness, a yearning for resolution and peace that seems unattainable. This incessant striving ironically hinders rest. When one's mind is overrun by such turmoil, one strays from the presence of God's provisions. It is in a state of perfect peace that we truly encounter the abundance of God's provisions. This is because the provisions of God meet a person when in perfect peace.

Understand this: a season of miracles has unfolded before you. What once was a struggle to attain will now be reached with ease and peace. There are two paths to these blessings: meekness and a lowliness of heart. Should a need arise, the Spirit of Christ may whisper to you, guiding you to seek help from another. When presented with such divine counsel, cast aside any semblance of pride and heed the call. Your mercy lies within this very act of reaching out and speaking up.

In moments where the Spirit prompts you to stand firm and witness the Lord's deliverance, hold your ground. Patience is key, for in your stillness, someone will emerge with the solution you seek. If impatience takes hold and you stray from your post, you may forfeit that destined encounter as the person designed to deliver your answer will find you absent.

Often, the chosen vessel for our provision remains unaware of his or her role in the divine plan. Just as the widow did not receive a nocturnal revelation of the prophet's impending visit, so too might your benefactor be oblivious to his or her charge. It is only by following the subtle impulses of the Spirit with impeccable timing that one shall not miss the sustenance ordained for him or her.

May the Grace of God ensure that your path to perfect peace is not marred by fear. In these challenging times, may the enveloping darkness not weigh upon your spirit. Instead, find solace in the profound truth that you have been called out of darkness into His marvellous light. We affirm once again that fears hold no sway, no dominion, over us. We are not shackled by fear but have embraced the Spirit of kinship. In calling out to our Heavenly Father, we find our strength. Fear shall not elicit a response from you, my readers. Only the deep recognition of our Father will stir your voices. Never shall desperation draw tears, for you are never forsaken or left without comfort from above. You have not received the spirit of bondage again to fear, but you have received the Spirit of adoption whereby you cry, 'Abba Father'. Lord, no fear will get a cry out of my readers. Only the knowledge of Abba will cause you to cry. There is no day that helplessness will cause you to cry because God will not leave you comfortless.

You have not received the spirit of bondage again to fear, but you have received the Spirit of adoption whereby you cry. 'Abba Father'. Let your name, Lord, be the only cry.

Printed in the United States
by Baker & Taylor Publisher Services